CALYX
BOOKS

The publication of this book was supported with grants from the Allen Foundation for the Arts, the Oregon Arts Commission, and The Robert M. Stafrin Fund of the Oregon Community Foundation. With grateful appreciation, CALYX acknowledges the following "Immortals" who provided substantial support for this book:

Nancy Dennis

Cheryl McLean

Cover art: "East Wind" by Katherine Ace. *Cover and book design:* Cheryl McLean

CALYX Books are distributed to the trade through Consortium Book Sales and Distribution, Inc., St. Paul, MN 1-800-283-3572.

CALYX Books are also available through major library distributors, jobbers, and most small press distributors including Airlift, Baker & Taylor, Banyan Tree, Bookpeople, Ingram, and Small Press Distribution. For personal orders or other information write: CALYX Books, PO Box B, Corvallis, OR 97339, (541) 753-9384, FAX (541) 753-0515.

∞

The paper in this book meets the guidelines for permanence and durability of the Committee on Production Guidelines for Book Longevity of the Council on Library Resources and the minimum requirements of the American National Standard for the Permanence of Paper for Printed Library Materials Z38.48-1984.

Library of Congress Cataloging-in-Publication Data

Cracking the earth: a 25th anniversary anthology from CALYX / edited by Beverly McFarland, Micki Reaman, Lois Cranston, Kristina Kennedy Daniels, Margarita Donnelly, Louise LaFond, Christine Rhea, Carolyn Sawtelle, Linda Varsell Smith, Sharilyn Smith

p. cm.

ISBN 0-934971-79-X (cl. : alk. paper) : $25.95. —ISBN 0-934971-78-1 (pbk. : alk. paper) : $12.95.

1. American literature—20th century. I. McFarland, Beverly. II. Reaman, Micki. III. CALYX, Inc.

PS536.2.C75 2001
810.8'09287'09045—dc21 2001035477

Printed in the U.S.A.

9 8 7 6 5 4 3 2 1

Cracking the Earth
A 25th Anniversary Anthology from CALYX

Edited by

Beverly McFarland, Senior Editor
Micki Reaman, Managing Editor
Lois Cranston
Kristina Kennedy Daniels
Margarita Donnelly
Louise LaFond
Christine Rhea
Carolyn Sawtelle
Linda Varsell Smith
Sharilyn Smith

CALYX BOOKS • CORVALLIS, OREGON

CRACKING THE EARTH:
A 25th Anniversary Anthology from CALYX

CONTENTS

PROSE

REVIEWS

CONTRIBUTORS' NOTES

PREFACE

CALYX is celebrating its twenty-fifth anniversary thanks to the generosity not only of the many writers and artists but also of the volunteers who donated their time and talent, their expertise and experience. While CALYX's mission is to nurture women writers and artists, the editors find they are nurtured as well by the work women send to CALYX. The number of volunteer editors participating in the collective has varied from the four original founders to up to eight editors. They have read every manuscript received over the years. Many of the editors have averaged five years, while some have continued to serve for ten and even twenty years, demonstrating their commitment to women's writing and art. We thank all the editors who through the years carefully read all the work received, then re-read the work that was held, and discussed the writing at the weekly meetings where the selections for publication—the hard decisions—were made.

We make a special acknowledgment to Lois Cranston, an exceptional editor, who spent ten years with CALYX and resigned in January due to ill health. Her generosity and commitment to women was demonstrated in the careful personal attention she gave to writers and to CALYX's vision. Thank you, Lois!

The editors who served throughout the twenty-five years: *Founding Editors:* Barbara Garden Baldwin, Margarita Donnelly, Meredith Jenkins, Elizabeth McLagan; ***Prose and Poetry Editors:*** Amy Agnello, Jo Alexander, Eva Bowman, Jan Caday, Yolanda Calvillo, Jo Cochran, Lois Cranston, Cathy Crawford, Luz Delgado, Lisa Domitrovich, Valerie Eames, Alice Ann Eberman, Bettina Escudero, Diane Glancy, Sonia Gomez, Rebecca Gordon, Katherine Gorham, Barbara Hadley, Donna Henderson, Patricia Herron, Catherine Holdorf, Anne Krosby, Jessica Lamb, Barbara Lewis, Shirley Geok-lin Lim, Susan Lisser, Dorothy Mack, Ruth Malone, Beverly McFarland, Laura McFarland, Cheryl McLean, Felicity Milner, Ann Mine, Naomi Littlebear Morena, Linda Morgan, Zola M. Mumford, Cynthia Orr, Carol Pennock, Emily Ransdell, Karen Ratté, Micki Reaman, Kathleen Reyes, Christine Rhea, Barbara Rohde, Beth Rosania, Teri Mae Rutledge, Michele Schuman, Mira Chieko Shimabukura, Vicki Shuck, Linda Varsell Smith, Sharilyn Smith, Maya Sonenberg, Sara Swanberg Spiegel, Ann Staley, Mary Tallmountain, Mayumi Tsutakawa, Sarah Williams, Eleanor Wilner, Michelle Wyrbeck; ***Art Editors:*** Debbie Berrow, Maria Francesca Braganza, Chris Carrol, Faye Cummins, Kristina Kennedy Daniels, Faylinda Kodis, Darryla Green-McGrath, Sutree Irving, Louise LaFond, Barbara Loeb, Ada Medina, Deb Ramsay, Carolyn Sawtelle, Vicki Shuck, Megan Smith.

INTRODUCTION

CALYX was founded twenty-five years ago, according to legend, as a temporary venue for women writers and artists. Margarita Donnelly tells me that its founding mothers were sure that, after five years, there would be no need for such a specialized journal. Yet we see that, with the vagaries of the publishing business, this work is more vital than ever.

And it *is* work. Anyone who has tried to raise money in the arts knows the dedication it takes to sustain such an effort. Blessed with brilliant blindness to the impossibility of its task, and a nurturing community of neighbors, patrons, writers, and arts organizations, CALYX continues to bring us the brightest of lights. In fact, CALYX consistently brings forth talent that sustains the wider fields of literature.

While CALYX was one of my first publishers, the collective rejected my stories just as regularly. Why was this? I didn't inundate them with work. I didn't include pictures of my cat or samples of my macramé or omit the dreaded SASE! With other journals, the pattern for me has been that either a publication accepts everything I send them or rejects everything—only CALYX seems to take each piece on its own merits.

This is for two reasons: CALYX is sought out by the most talented writers in the country, and accepts only the best. The CALYX collective, through the years and changes in literary fashion and emphasis, has remained extremely selective. The women included in this twenty-fifth anniversary anthology should be very pleased, both with the evident quality of their work and the literary company they are keeping.

Cracking the Earth is full of ghosts—of lives lost, of deaths unavenged or unacknowledged. It is full of the voices that we cannot hear, as Frances Payne Adler says, until we have "cracked the dry earth of silence." These writers are women who do not hesitate to wear either their gender or their politics on their sleeves. Most of all, this anthology is full of the ghosts of lives unrealized, from that of the very sexy ghost in Diana Ma's "Ghost Story" to the young girl in Susan Vreeland's "Neptune's Lung" and the increasingly mad housewife in Monique de Varennes' "Cabeza."

Searching for a phrase that spoke from the heart of this anthology, I found it in "Rainbows and Roses" by Elaine Winer:

> *I get a feeling of how hard that concrete really is, and I sense below the concrete the whole solid earth, the layers of rock, the fire at the center, the enormity of a planet turning in space, all beneath my left foot. And I know it's big enough to support one skinny old woman.*

CALYX grounds us in the things that matter. With this anniversary anthology, we find that she has not lost her touch, nor will she allow us to forget the reason for literature—to make us understand that *we* can crack the earth and change the world.

KATHLEEN ALCALÁ
BAINBRIDGE ISLAND, WA
SPRING 2001

The Voices Are Coming Up

In the first years of the twenty-first century, it was discovered
that voices, all the unheard ones, didn't die at the end of life.
Instead, they spent thousands of years, wandering underground.
... It was an earthquake like no other....
Frances Payne Adler, from *Raising the Tents*

for Julie Bliss, in search of Mary Garner Cole, 1863–1939

You are a search party traveling back for your great
grandmother, for years you've been studying Choctaw,
you hear faint directions cracking open, you track them back,
uncover them in ditches of history books, the songs the whispers
of family stories, a name, a date, a town inscribed in a bible,
a page in a diary, homestead documents in a thin drawer,
calling you under the canyons the coasts of California to
Iowa to Missouri, and in your face the clocks are clanging
the docks banging together, wind, waves, and fluid fields
of corn hang over hang under you, you pitch the tents of your
questions. *Grandmother, speak to me*, you say, and you can hear
her, calling you back for the voices, for the years she's been
chanting Choctaw, not stripped from your family, not lost
to the conquerers, not lost to marriage nor to gods, she's calling
you, your great grandmother, knowing you've retrieved the eyes
to see her, the ears to hear her, her words, to have them surface
the centuries, the years between you, you will crack the dry earth
of silence, tell the stories she hands you, broken stories no longer,
no longer leeched of her truth, her blood no longer sapped from you

Frances Payne Adler

A Call to Arms and Breast Cancer

"What possible choices do most of us have in the air we breathe and the water we must drink?"
Poet Audre Lorde, who died in 1992 after fifteen years of living
with breast and liver cancer, from *A Burst of Light*

"In 2000, one in eight women developed breast cancer, compared with one in 14 in 1960."
National Cancer Institute, 2000

"Women with the highest exposure to the pesticide DDT have four times the breast cancer risk."
Mary S. Wolff, PhD., chemist, Mount Sinai School of Medicine, NY

She grew up eating berries beans apples and peas and stuffed her bra with socks
She grew up eating grapes and greens, and on TV, breasts sold beer and cars and
musk perfume, jeans and jewels and junket tours, breasts and chests
and marketing plans, these golden globs, these silken globes
It sinks in early this thing with breasts, sinks into her

through apples coated with poison, poisons sliding down her throat
to her breasts, spreading like fingers along the milk route
Breast cancer, they tell her, we have to cut it off, they say, and they do,
and someone is singing *chest bust bosom tits chest bust bosom tits*

And they talk to her of fitting her for a fake one, No one will ever know, they say
Know? she says, *I want everyone to know, I want to run up and up the streets*
calling to women wearing prostheses, to yank them from their chests, to scatter
them on sidewalks, let everyone see us one-breasted women, millions of us

How long are we going to go on killing women, she says, a chant, *how long*,
a prayer she murmurs as she slips in and out of sleep, *killing women*, her kidneys
giving out, her liver giving out, yellowing her skin, leaving her itchy, scratching
at her flesh, longing to get out of it and on to a world that makes some sense

And in her deathdream, breast cancer researchers collect the tossed prostheses,
trade them in like used bottles for gold from corporations who made millions
from all the cars from all the beer that breasts sold

FRANCES PAYNE ADLER

And the Eyes of the Blind Shall Be Opened

It's all I can do not to stray from the high
holy Latin to the risen Christ, flanked by disciples,
ascending, or are they descending above the altar,
above the anorexic Jesus racked to the cross.

This scene like a meditation of things to come,
between the bells and candles and incense
of my blind faith, but it's not the resurrected face
I contemplate so much as the drape of cloth

that billows about Him like a pregnancy.
And I worry about the way His feet flap below
the ankles like the feet of a hanged man or my own
when I hung on the school yard monkey bars

mouthing all the dirty words I knew.
I remember our Baptist pastor, his gap-toothed grin
and mousy exhausted wife, the evidence
of their sexual life stair-stepping the front pew.

Our bodies were empty vessels, he said, and I thought
of my mother's milk-glass pitcher, hobnailed
with small, aggressive breasts, and of my own body, tipped
so the flames could drain from my eyes, my mouth,

the tips of my fingers. And Jesus would fill me
as mist pours into trees or ice numbs my mouth
until my words would slur into ecstasy. Even now
it's not that I wouldn't want to be one of the disciples,

ascend the strung-out laundry of sky, let the wind
bend my back into a curve and be filled
with something that swells with the light
to come. *She*, I still whisper, when we name

the Holy Spirit, though it's harder to follow
the Latin mutter. There's a moth somewhere, wakened
from darkness. I feel it flutter against me, against
the bright weight of all I am not supposed to say.

ELIZABETH MCLAGAN

THE LITURGY OF THE TABLE

for my mother

I can't write about you until you are dead
I want to tell her. Until you have become
a philosophy instead of a religion.

I can't write about you as Mother
with food as your savior child:
your love always bubbling in the oven.

You would cry if you read that. Say
I loved my life. Say *I loved your father*.
Say *I loved serving*.

You taught me well: to love in our religion
is to never say anything.
I remember that as I stir chocolate chips

into the cookies
my child waits for as if
I was going to say something.

BETSY JOHNSON-MILLER

Altar Living

My father says he will make the arrangements
since I am returning home. My mother's ashes
have been hanging around the house
too long. Thirteen years of altar living:
evolving ordinary objects into offerings
because that is all we can do.

Table, white cloth, vase, and flowers.
Bowls of food. A photograph of her.
A piece of wood, painted in characters
I can't understand, but I know spell
her name, the same way that ribbons
of apple peel thrown over my shoulder
spell out the future. I've lived
with ash longer than living body
but let me tell you, this heavy
metal urn has been cool comfort in summer.

Some days her name was a river
when I pressed my cheek against
the engraved box of her body.
Other days the sharp corners
were all that stayed in focus
as I felt my way back to the present.

Returning back to the earth is not an easy thing.
How can I understand holding
on and letting go when the only thing
my hands can do is shake off the dust
the years have gathered.

Janine H. Oshiro

You Know Her

She is a wooden beam of a woman
so stiff you could prop the entire Southern
Baptist Church against her hips

and still she would not fall.
Yeah, she's the woman who cracked
the jar, but she won't take the blame

for what spilled out. Her gods,
if you could find them, would not
allow young men to graduate

into the schooled arms of war, nor
let a young girl's permanent teeth
rot in a country where insurance is

the safety net with man-size holes.
When a life bleeds out of her body
she doesn't have time to weep.

All night she dishes up eggs-over-easy
at the Bye-N-Bye Truck Stop. All day in a factory
she guts chickens for America's white meat.

Don't speak to her of the wages of sin.
Don't talk motherhood to a woman who's spent
her life, so far, nursing every child but her own.

Jane Bailey

CEASEFIRE

for Sothreaksa

It is enough to listen now
to the long vowels of the surf

and look at the waves
which are forever

teaching stones how to soften
the natural curves of their backs.

It is enough to be a girl again who bends
to pick something up without thinking

about the waves of blue-green
armies that erase the lines

drawn painstakingly in sand
and mortared into the deep

space that separates Us from Them.
Her parents lean against piled bones

of driftwood, watching the wind
turn cartwheels in her hair.

The sun, fractured by high clouds,
is brighter than it has a right to be.

The girl's face, a secret agent, reveals
no clues to her dreams.

Are there soldiers? Are there storms?
Down the road, the future

waits to see what a daughter of war
will take away from the detritus—

a small rock she can break with her hands
or a perfect ear-shaped shell that roars

but will not in a million years explode.

JANE BAILEY

ANNE

when Billy Collins said, you can't really write
about the Holocaust

In the nights of insomnia I read
Anne Frank's new biography
and even wading through this crush
of authenticated facts, her portrait
since birth, nothing changes
from the diary itself. A bright,
talkative, hard-to-handle, audacious,
obnoxious teenager, bordering on genius,
is going to die—faceless—at the end.

Her father, who didn't send her to England
three weeks before the Nazi trap was sprung
because he couldn't bear to part with her,
sees her the last time in a selection line.

She has her clothes then. Later, head shaved,
pubic hair shaved, her beautiful innocence revealed—
which wanted in all good time
a bed lit with afternoon sun,
one sweet article of clothing after the next,
a boy just that naïve
and head over heels in love.

My sleepless brain refuses the lists
of details—where Anne's mother's brothers are in the U.S.,
that second cousin in Switzerland,
the year the Nazis made the Jews stay home after 8 p.m.,
the year they weren't allowed into movie theaters,
the year they couldn't ride bikes, couldn't own bikes,
the year 569,355 yellow stars were issued—a small galaxy—
the step-by-step squeeze
which wasn't
wasn't death.

Smart and aware, Otto chose the wrong country—
that's all, something he couldn't have known.

For me, sleep, so long evasive,
suddenly appears: *take me now or forget it*,
and I switch out the light—
prized, courted sleep—
the sleep I slept at her age—
the way my daughter sleeps now—
heavy, unshakable,
mornings forever.

Daylight. I wake in a sweat;
each noise brings a new wave
of hot and cold.
Get up. Get up.
But the heavy limbs won't go into my clothes,
I can't get breakfast, everything's burning,

and my daughter,
my entering teenage daughter,
I don't put my arms around her
but gaze at her from the line
I'm forbidden to cross, the place
from which I can never save her

even if I rush the line
and the bullet doesn't take me from behind.

Alice Derry

Reprieve

It's his first day off in weeks:
coffee at Peets on Fourth Street.
Sunday afternoon with his lover.
For ten years he tended dying men
and now he splints the broken struts of wings,
checks blood for parasites and toxins, checks
weight. The oiled birds have piled up on the shore
in thousands, black and gleaming bodies
lining the beach. They have worked
desperately at their coated feathers
and now the thick oil clogs their gut.
Although it's easier to change an IV
than flush out a wild duck that hisses and stabs
with its flat bill, there's nothing querulous
about a sick bird: it lives, protesting, or lies
acquiescent, the white membranous eyelids
flicked up. What's different is not the scale,
but knowing some are going to make it.
These ones begin to preen again, zipping
the barbs of their feathers with their beaks,
fluffing the white down. Freed on the shore,
they wheel from him over the water,
their wings whistling.

Jasmine Donahaye

Nunca Tu Alma

I turn my eyes from the girls' thin bodies
in Sarajevo and from the corpses that float downriver
like matchsticks, but here in the clinic
I sit with Maya—a twelve year old, raped
by her sister's friend—who asks me *Am I still a virgin?*
I examine her crimson vagina. Three
delicate tears lace her perineum, as if Maya
has had a rough delivery.
I culture for GC, chlamydia, draw blood
for pregnancy, HIV.
Am I still a virgin? she asks, her voice disembodied
above her knees, bent and open,
her hips narrow as a boy's beneath the sheet.
I struggle with *mechanical/emotional*, consider
the penis as metaphor. When we're finished,
Maya and I lean close, face to face.
Virginity is a matter of love, I say, when you give yourself
out of joy. Rape takes only your body, never your soul.
Maya nods, repeats this in Spanish
to her mother and sister, three dark women
singing like birds. Maya imitates me, her fist
strikes her palm. *Nunca, nunca tu alma.*
Her tests are negative.
Maya's more like thirty than twelve,
the nurse whispers, and I agree.
I crumple her sheet and dump the bloody swabs.
Shove the metal stirrups into the table, out of sight.

Cortney Davis

IT IS AUGUST 24TH

and at last I'm leaving the clinic
with its faded paint, its finally empty waiting room.
Good-bye to the women and their screaming children,
good-bye to the pregnant blonde whose water
broke early at twenty-five weeks
after a coke binge she finally confessed to.
I'm leaving that tone in my voice
as I probed her vagina and quoted statistics of loss,
her uterus foul with bacteria. *From what?*
I wanted to ask. *From an all night party, his oily fingers?*

Walking into the sun past "Women's Health,"
past the dried scum on the pavement
where they scuff out their smokes,
tear gum wrappers into a hundred paper swans—
on my tax money, I say later to friends, *on my tax money*—
my skin lets go of that blonde, the bloody water
that blasted apart her thighs, filling my shoes
as I opened, carefully, with one hand's fingers
the bluish lips. I think about her as I pass a man
dressed in a no-color sweatshirt, his eyes
twin blue stones.
He says *Hi*, so low I almost turn.

I'm used to being polite
to every patient who looks into my eyes
as if they were my friend, so I answer
Hi, and walk on. There is the soft suck of gum soles
as he falls in behind me, the sound
like sticky amniotic fluid drying on the floor.
After her exam, the woman lay back
and drew up her knees. I'm better than her,

I thought, as I dropped the speculum
into the bucket, peeled off my latex gloves,
hands pale, knuckles without her jail-blue tattoos.
I know this is hard, I said,
in that way one woman has
when she turns away from another woman.

Suck, suck, our shadows walk,
light wavering around us like the fringe of flesh
that rings the vagina. What should I do?
Walk faster? Turn to stare? Run
to the alarm box, the security man, wondering
how *he* feels today,
how much better than me as I punch the buzzer
once, twice, over and over?
I see the woman in the clinic
turn toward me, eyeliner like thumbprints
under her eyes. I say *The baby*
will probably not survive.
This is some fucking mess, she says, my car
on the far side of the ramp, the man
right behind me, both of us knowing
that I am a woman
like any woman—
just skin and hair and that sharp primal cry.

CORTNEY DAVIS

Apology to Anne

In 1991 The False Memory Syndrome Foundation was formed by parents accused of child sexual abuse and professionals who deny the veracity of survivors' memories. Anne Sexton's former psychiatrist, Martin Orne, is a member of their board of directors. As co-author of The Courage to Heal, *I have been one of their targets.*

The arrow of time never reverses. The broken glass
does not rise up onto the table, composing
its jagged pieces as lovers
might pat themselves back into place
at the end of a stolen afternoon. You are dead
these twenty-five years and I cannot help you.
But the irony of time's strict rules
still troubles me. I was too young
when we sat in your kitchen and you fed me
encouragement like rich egg custard to an invalid.
Write more. Expand! you urged, your silver blue
eyes looking right into mine. Then
I can't be in the sun, as you lifted a pale
elegant arm to the bright back yard—*the medicine*.
Like a child husband in a royal marriage,
I was incapable of offering anything.

Too late, I know what to say
when women open their pocketbooks of pain.
Together we turn the rage and fear—those twin
socks of despair—inside out. Secrets
huddled like hungry children
creep out and blink in the light.

If you could have waited just a little longer—
the times were changing. Seventy-one—
and what poems you'd be making from the lives
of all your gathered selves.

How I wish I could go back and dethrone
the one who wouldn't recognize those thin
terrified voices, who couldn't believe
the splintering of children's minds
when those they love reach in with fists—
like gutting a holiday turkey.

I would have listened to every
night crying bleakly within you.
I would have held those cries in my hands, raw
like the ripped yolks and whites of broken eggs.
Before your suffering was pieced and glued
into poems, when it was still all
slime and bits of sharp shell,
I would have held you.

ELLEN BASS

Farthest Thoughts

Mummy fragments were stolen, broken up
and crushed into powder which was sold as
an aphrodisiac well into the 18th *century.*
From *The Search for Ancient Egypt*

No stone husband. No clay lovers.
She's been left with alabaster servants
to face the length of death. Buried
with hundreds of lapis doppelgangers,
all smaller than her, they'll never help.
Someone *(who could it have been?)*
had a crocodile embalmed, as if this
would have made things easier. Maybe
whispered by a concubine
her husband bathed with, or the priest
who performed trephination,
boring a hole in her head
with his obsidian knife,
they'd have thought, *she needs*
all the luck she can get.
She lies stiff with love or rigid
with fear among baskets of scarabs—
until Bedouin women rob her tomb.
Armed with magic formulas to outwit spirits,
their brains tingle with jubilant thoughts
of what they can sell, while hers rest
in a jar just out of reach.

Deborah Byrne

INSOMNIA

MARINA TSVETAEVA

Translated from the Russian by KRISTIN BECKER

1

For me—insomnia—eyes
Ringed with dark shadow.
For me—insomnia—a dark crown
Twines the eyes.

That's what comes of nights
Praying to idols!
I've betrayed your secret,
Idolatress.

The day, the sun's fire,
Is not enough for you!

Wear a pair of my rings,
Paleness!
You have summoned
The dark wedding crown.

Has your call meant so little?
Has our sleep meant so little?

You'll lie down with a still, blank face.
People will bow to you.
I'll be your lector,
Insomnia:

—Sleep, my peace,
Sleep, your honor,
Sleep, my crowned
Woman.

So your sleep will come easy,
I'll be your cantor:

—Sleep, tireless
Friend!
Sleep, little pearl,
Sleep, sleeplessness.

Forget the letters we've written
And the vows we've made…
Sleep now.

At last separations—
Dissolve.
At last your hands—
Release your hands.
There now, at last, your struggle has ended,
Sweet martyr.

Sleep is holy.
Everyone's asleep.
The crown—removed.

2

Hands—I love
To kiss them, and I love
To give out names,
And what's more—to throw
Doors open wide
Into the dark night!

I've pressed my head
To hear a heavy step
Fade off somewhere,
As the wind shakes
The sleepy, sleepless
Woods.

Ah, night!
Somewhere streams are running.
I'm drowsy—
Almost asleep.
Somewhere in the night
A person is drowning.

3

In my enormous city—night.
I leave my sleeping home—flight.
And people think: daughter, wife—
While I remember only: night.

The July wind sweeps my road
And there's music in some window—low.
Ah, till dawn the wind will blow
Through the chest's thin walls—to the soul.

A black poplar, and through the window—light.
A bell on the tower, and in my hand—a flower.
Here is my footstep—no one before me—
And here is my shadow—but no me.

Lights—like threads of golden beads.
In my mouth the taste of night's leaves.
From the bonds of day, set me free,
And understand, my friends—I come to you in dreams.

4

After a sleepless night the body grows weak,
Becomes sweet and not your own—nobody's.
Yet in the sluggish veins aching arrows swim—
And you smile at people, like the seraphim.

After a sleepless night the arms grow weak,
And both enemy and friend deeply indifferent.
A whole rainbow appears in each chance sound,
And the frost smells suddenly of Florence.

The lips glow softly, the shadow under the sunken eyes
Turns gold. This night has lit up
This brightest face—and the dark night
Darkens just one part of it—the eyes.

5

Now I'm a heavenly guest
In your country.
I've seen the forest's insomnia
And the sleep of the fields.

Somewhere in the night horseshoes
Plowed through the grass.
A cow sighed heavily
In the sleeping barn.

I will tell you with sadness,
With all gentleness,
About the guard-goose
And the sleeping geese.

Hands sank in dog hair.
The dog was—gray.
Then, toward six—
Daybreak.

6

Tonight I am alone in the night—
A sleepless, homeless nun!—
Tonight I have the keys to all
The gates of the one and only capital.

Insomnia has pushed me to walk the paths.
—My tarnished Kremlin, you're so beautiful!—
Tonight I kiss the breast
Of the whole round warring earth.

What rises isn't hair—but fur,
And the stifling wind blows straight to the soul.
Tonight I pity everyone—
Those who pity and those who kiss.

7

Softly softly, gently gently,
Something whistled in the pines.
I saw a dark-eyed baby
In a dream of mine.

So hot sap drips
From the pine in the woods.
So in my fine night
A saw crosses my heart.

8

Black like a pupil, like a pupil sucking
Light—I love you, sharp-sighted night.

Give me the voice to sing of you, first mother
Of songs, in your palms—the bridle of four winds.

Calling to you, praising you, I'm only
A shell, in which the ocean resounds.

Night! I've seen enough of the human
Eye! Burn me up, black sun—night!

9

Who sleeps at night? Nobody sleeps!
An infant in its cradle screams,
An old man mulls over his death,
Whoever is young talks with his love,
Eyes fixed on her eyes, breath mixed with her breath.

Fall asleep—and will you ever wake here again?
We'll have time time time to sleep!

Door to door with his rose-colored torch,
The vigilant watchman goes,
And over the pillows with staccato thunder
His furious clapper roars:

—Don't sleep! Be strong! It's for your own good!
Otherwise—eternal sleep! Otherwise—eternal home!

10

A window yet again
Where yet again there's no sleep.
Maybe—they're drinking wine,
Maybe—they just sit.
Or simply—two pairs of hands
Joined, persist.
In each home, my friend,
There's a window like this.

A cry of meetings and farewells—
You, window in the night!
Maybe—hundreds of candles,
Maybe—three lights…
To my mind there comes no
Peace, no rest.
And in my home
It has become like this.

Pray, dear friend, for the sleepless home,
And for the flame-lit window.

MARINA TSVETAEVA
Translated from the Russian by KRISTIN BECKER

TEA PARTY WITH OPEN FRUIT — 44" X 36" alkyd/oil — KATHERINE ACE

If there were one overriding thematic connection in my work, it would be contradiction. I find that I'm curious about the struggles of diversity vs. unity in human, animal, and plant societies. I am captivated by complex issues that we all face, and all experience as deeply personal. I am interested in the role of dark feelings, thoughts, and states of mind in the process of transformation. I am drawn to fire beneath reserve.

All art included in this anthology was selected from the 25th Anniversary Art Show at the Corvallis Arts Center, March 2001.

BIRDIE | 14"H x 6" x 5" | IGGI GREEN

mixed media sculpture

Courtesy of Froelick Gallery

These soft sculptures' detailed fetishes, fingernails, and eyeballs juxtapose contemporary taxidermy materials with traditional fabrics. Like Frankenstein's monster, a sewn skin of asymmetrical patterned and textured material conveys different parts of the body. The teeth evidence a fascination with Francis Bacon. The imperfect human forms are grotesque, coincidentally both scary and funny.

IN SEARCH FOR THE ULTIMATE ROACH JOKE 17"H X 5" X 20" mixed media GAIL TREMBLAY

"In Search for the Ultimate Roach Joke" is a piece about how words have particular cultural meanings that can lead to cross-cultural misunderstandings that are sometimes quite ironic and humorous. The most common usage for the word roach *in the indigenous communities of the plains is the porcupine fur and eagle feather headdress worn by traditional dancers at powwows. For housewives in older neighborhoods it is most commonly used for the ubiquitous cockroach they wish to eliminate from their lives. For aging hippies remembering their youths, it is the butt of a marijuana cigarette. A single word can bring up very different associations for different people and create less communication rather than more.*

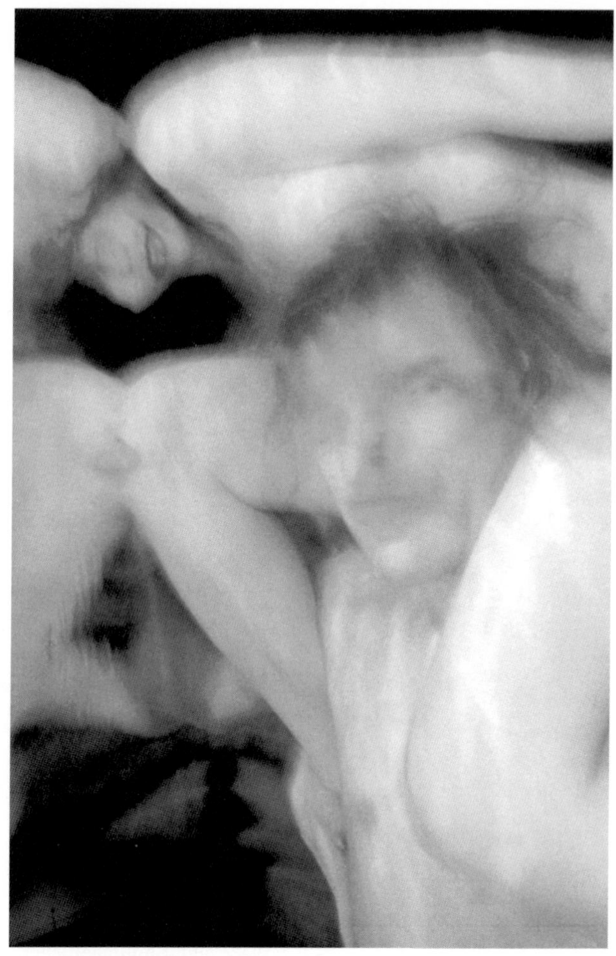

OCCUPYING HIMSELF WITH HER 16" X 20" photography SHELLY CORBETT

I have been photographing underwater for over ten years. The imagery of my work is a manipulation of neutral elements—water, light, lenses, film—with the spontaneous action of the models and props. I do not impose on them any set of desires or expectations but rather pursue what people are up to under their skins—to illustrate that thin line in all of us that moves between the proverbial love and hate, pleasure and pain, in a highly individualistic way. It's a mystery that is amplified through the use of an underwater theater.

GETAWAY — 7" X 9" X 3" mixed media — SHERI RICE

In the harmonious spirit of art and recycling, my work combines the unexpected; this way of collecting and working allows me a continuous creative adventure.

I found this rusty roller skate in Kingman, Arizona, and right away I thought "Freedom," an important theme for me. I added wings and "diamonds" and a silk stand to make "Getaway."

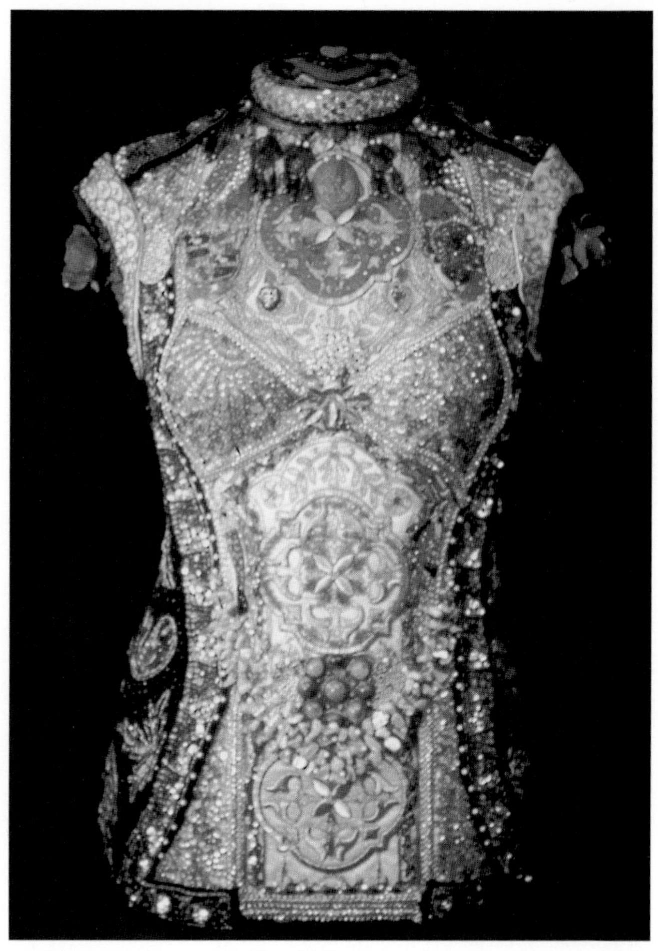

QUEEN OF HEARTS 15" X 32" JENNIFER STABLER HOLLAND
found object sculpture

Because of my work as an artist and proprietor of an antique shop, I started receiving articles about antique art forms and folk art and craft. One day I saw a piece about "memory jars"—old vases completely encrusted with mementos of a deceased loved one—pieces of dishes, jewelry, photos—the detritus of that person's life. At the same time I kept seeing craft projects using broken jewelry and shells. I had a molded body dress form at the store, and all the pieces came together. The "Corpus Memento" series began. The bodies were autobiographical at first, but have now branched out and refer to women of history and other cultures.

JADE VASE 38" X 44" CHI MEREDITH
oil on canvas
Courtesy of Alysia Duckler Gallery, Portland

This painting comes from the period of time when I was exploring interiors and architecture settings of the home. In looking for images of interest, I was intrigued by the use of vases and pottery in these settings. Painting these vases larger than life was a way to draw attention to the casual placement of vases and other objects spread quietly around the interior or exterior of an office or home. I also wanted to emphasize the solidity and beauty of form in the environment. As with any art object that speaks for itself, the painting of that object then becomes an echo of the original form. It forces the viewer (and painter) to see the object with new eyes.

LITTLE BLACK DRESS 26" X 39" MANYA SHAPIRO
paper and pins

My work is influenced by women's traditional crafts and domestic art (quilting, sewing, weaving, basketry). My process is like a dialogue with materials that have powerful associations for me. Dresses are evocative of the figure, but also speak of women's body image, cultural roles, and rituals. As I create these symbolic dresses, I hope to arouse memories or narratives in the viewer of a real or imagined past or future.

ERITREA: WAR HARVEST — 33" X 45" acrylic — BETTY LADUKE

This village mother (a universal Madonna) echoes the duality of hope and suffering as she holds a millet stalk in her hand containing winged-seeds that soar upward—symbolizing a vision of peace. However, her skirt is filled with spirit memories of young lives sacrificed in a defensive war against the Ethiopian invasion 1998-2000.

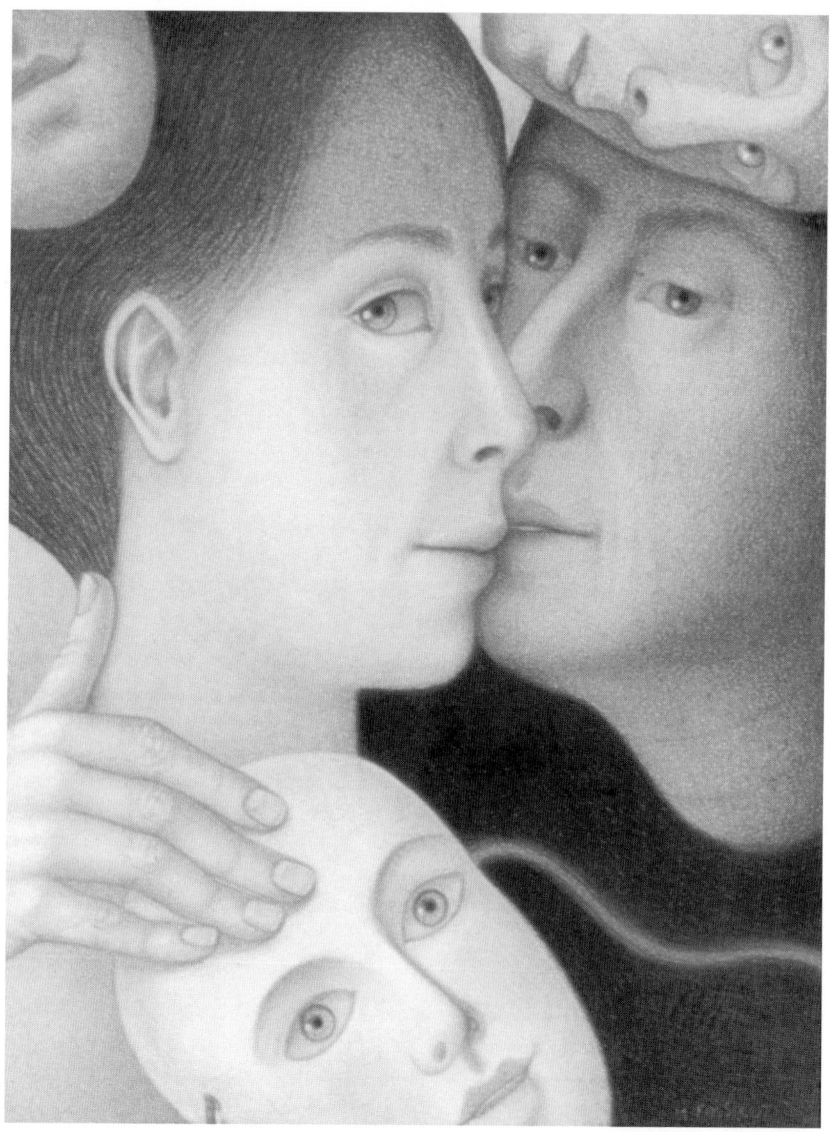

THE RED RIBBON MASK 12" X 16" MONIQUE PASSICOT
colored pencils/graphite

My work is never about definitions or reaching a final meaning. All it offers is a certain way of looking at things.

WAITING 22" X 43" ANGELITA SURMON
acrylic on handmade paper

My work is all autobiographical in one way or another. The current body of work revolves around the importance of relationships, the fragility and brevity of life, and the importance of living in the moment.

THE CENTAUR 23" X 27" ANNETTE GURDJIAN
oil and wax on photograph

I work with the visual interplay between the mediums of painting and photography. Sometimes the photograph becomes the canvas atop which I paint. At other times I use photographs in my paintings on paper and masonite, integrating them into the final painting. While painting, I am continually responding both visually and emotionally to the photographic images that I am using. The degree to which the photograph appears in its original form in the finished painting varies. Sometimes it is only the outer shape that matters, the photographic image disappearing completely under the paint. Mine is an intuitive and interactive process.

HEAR NO EVIL, SEE NO EVIL, SPEAK NO EVIL 18" X 14" oil JANE ORLEMAN

The primary focus of my work is the exploration of psychological reality through symbolic narrative imagery. I concentrate on events in my personal world—past and present—sifting though these events to find their meaning. In the process, experiences, feelings, and intentions may become transformed, creating new possibilities. This intuitive process, my choice of symbols and colors, and the inner world that I explore all combine to create paintings that express my distinctly female worldview. Openness to this inner dialogue has created the visual evidence detailing a journey of self-discovery.

PALMISTRY — 12" X 14" collage — JOANNA THOMAS

Because of my passion for poetry, often my visual art is inspired by language. Words provide an armature for me, around which I can build a series of images. This body of work—titled "Bud, Bark, Twig"—consists of a dozen pieces, all of which play on the sound of the word tree. *Some individual pieces are "Palmistry," "Symmetry," "Deviltry," "Tapestry," and "Gentry." I am endlessly fascinated to discover such a thread in language and to see just how far I can follow it.*

BLOWEN IN THE WIND — 20" X 13" gouache on paper — CLAUDIA CAVE

Since childhood, I have experienced a rich dream life that has influenced my studio work. When dreaming, the mind releases its grip, allowing images to flow freely, without the usual limitations. I use a similar process when approaching a new painting, opening my mind and imagination and releasing as much as possible my waking logical or rational will. Often unusual image combinations emerge, just as in a dream, disclosing symbolic messages from the unconscious.

PAINTED TRILLIUM | 42" X 42" oil on canvas | KRISTINA KENNEDY DANIELS

I am interested in light and color, the immediacy and physical richness of the paint and the meaningful juxtaposition of seemingly disparate images. A successful balance among these preoccupations can result in a coherent and expressive narrative. Painting is a communicative activity.

Made of Crêpe de Chine

A needle running in white crêpe de chine
Is not the frail servant of utility
It was designed to be;
It is an arrow of silver sunlight
Plunging with a waterfall.

And hands moving in white crêpe de chine
Are not slaves of the precedent
That governs them;
They are the crouching women of a fountain,
Who have sprung from marble into life
To bathe ecstatically
In the brimming basin.

Hazel Hall

A Baby's Dress

It is made of finest linen—
Sheer as wasp-wings;
It is made with a flowing panel
Down the front,
All overrun with fagot-stitched bow-knots
Holding hours and hours
Of fairy-white forget-me-nots.

And it is finished.
To-night, crisp with new pressing,
It lies stiffly in its pasteboard box,
Smothered in folds of tissue paper
Which envelop it like a shroud—
In its coffin-shaped pasteboard box.

To-morrow a baby will wear it at a christening;
To-morrow the dead-white of its linen
Will glow with the tint of baby skin;
And out of its filmy mystery
There will reach
Baby hands…

But to-night the lamplight plays over it and finds it cold.
Like the flower-husk of a little soul,
Which, new-lived, has fluttered to its destiny,
It lies in its coffin-shaped pasteboard box.

To-morrow will make it what hands cannot:
Limp and warm with babyness,
A hallowed thing,
A baby's dress.

Hazel Hall

Maker of Songs

Take strands of speech, faded and broken;
Tear them to pieces, word from word,
Then take the ravelled shreds and dye them
With meanings that were never heard.

Place them across the loom. Let wind-shapes
And sunlight come in at the door,
Or let the radiance of raining
Move in silver on the floor.

And sit you quiet in the shadow
Before the subtly idle strands.
Silence, a cloak, will weigh your shoulder;
Silence, a sorrow, fill your hands.

Yet there shall come the stirring… Weaver,
Weave well and not with words alone;
Weave through the pattern every fragment
Of glittered breath that you have known.

Hazel Hall

Closeted Lesbian Infiltrates Latvian Knitters' Group

All the women are frankly curious,
their eyes light up at my *labdien.*
Cast on two hundred twenty stitches.

A new face. *Miller? Miller? You wouldn't*
be Doctor Miller's daughter? Oh, you're not?
Increase one stitch at end of next two rows.

It's not your maiden name? You've lived
here how long? Twenty years already?
Put half the stitches on a holder, knit the rest.

Don't think I've ever seen you at the Latvian House.
Which congregation would you be in?
Knit two together, make one, two together.

I'm the black sheep. I married wrong.
I didn't send my kids to Latvian school.
Repeat the pattern eight more times.

I didn't come to church. I never joined
the Latvian choir or went to song fests.
Cast off ten center stitches.

It's bad enough that I'm a vegetarian.
There's more to come, for I'm a lesbian too.
Decrease two stitches next ten rows.

If I were shy I'd turn into a mouse
and run away. But I'm enjoying this.
Knit two, purl two, repeat till end of row.

How nice to be the focus of attention—
excitement surges round the room.
Increase ten stitches spacing evenly.

And sitting here among my grizzled
contemporaries, how young I feel!
Purl twelve, turn work, knit twelve.

We could have all been schoolmates, wives
and mothers, going through life together.
Work even from the chart until the end.

You followed old recipes, made Latvian
cheese, baked yellow saffron bread.
Work thirty stitches, place on holder.

I went to demonstrations, walked
in Gay Pride marches, tried to be p.c.
Follow Chart B, work back and forth.

What difference does it make? The needles
click, we sit companionably together.
Work knit rows right to left and purl rows left to right.

Without great urgency our talk unrolls
like yarn, familiar words in our familiar tongue.
Break yarn, pass through last stitch. Repeat for other side.

ILZE KLAVIŅA MUELLER

My Super Bowl

January 28th. Ninety percent of North America is obsessed
with Ravens & Giants. Just the time to mention this:
in the football game of our love, it's always first and goal.
Continual scoring. We can't seem to lose. Coin toss:

it's us! Shoot the moon on a Hail Mary: we score!
"Nervy," the commentators say, but we're golden;
every time we take a flyer, we chalk up
another six. If we like the feel of three,

we kick, and the ball clears the posts so clean,
it lands in the arms of an ecstatic six-year-old
on the upper deck, out of her seat for the kick.
She makes a perfect catch, then flushes,

an electric flush, thrilling. She keeps the ball close
for the remainder of the game, running a finger
over the laces' imprint on her arm; all through the game,
she can hear the thrum of the ball.

Years later, someone she's beginning to love
will see the ball in a corner of her room
and ask her if she used to play. She'll tell her
about the game, about the ball lifting into the air,

about knowing it was headed straight for her open arms.
It is late afternoon; their bodies, released, still pulse
with spin; the world reads wide open, like a field,
like a ball streaming up, like everything knows

exactly where it's going. As the air slips through
the unguarded zone between afternoon and evening,
the girl who made the catch drifts toward the other
and begins again the pleasure of skin and limb.

Belinda Kremer

Paradise

There's a pig in it, snuffling among the olive trees,
though I don't see her during the eternal moment
nor will I ever see her in this particular
eternal moment on the warm rock
by the river, since you can't shift around
in an eternal moment
once it's started.

I was expecting bears to come down
though the woods, from the hill on my left
and cross over in front of me
as I headed toward the river
at the bottom of the ravine.
We make a good pattern together in these dreams.
But today the path is strangely silent.

Then I sit and sit on the warm rock
where I can see the top of my head
from wherever I am, high in memory, or sleep.
Now the terraces are covered with wild grass,
the old gardens held up by piles of ancient stones.
I see from all angles,
see water running over stones in dappling shadows,
get light mixed up with sound, feel something that
is beyond happy, translates as mild nausea
of falling in, of falling in
so hard to find again, an angel
must have his foot against the gate.

Anita Sullivan

Mother and Son Negotiate

It might be possible for one or two of our worlds
to link up if we act discreetly
in the manner of Mongolian bandits
conducting transactions of dubious honor
in an abandoned fortress of stone
north of the Silk Road, silent under the
sprawling stars. Not necessary
to trust each other.
We are cloaked, and I whisper, "Yes!
it is that one, see!" pointing to a silver
bar of moonlight on the dirt floor.
For me this is the same as the rainbow
I drove through earlier today
with your brother, and we spoke
of how rare and fine it is to see
a rainbow from beneath.
You shake your head, "That light
is *numbered!*" you sneer, I nod. Light
is non-negotiable. So we sit
for a century and feel time
drift along our eyelids and hearts
as cool sand made out of millions
of silver filings from this treasure
on the floor. Could I try to tell you

how, in another of my worlds,
your head keeps appearing
above a certain wall? I know your name.
I pass through this desert now and then, could leave you
that world in plain
brown paper, depending on how well the moon
has shed during the previous year,
what color is leaping up
at the base of the mountains. And more, and more.
But I can barely see you, a figure
shivering.

ANITA SULLIVAN

Provider

You will be well provided for, Father said and said.
But Mother and I never suspected there'd be
twenty thousand cash in the back of a file drawer.
Hundred dollar bills, the wad held together
with dry rubber bands cracking in our hands.

I figured I understood his reasons: early manhood
during the Depression, the Liebowitz real estate business
belly up, dazed Jewish refugees sleeping in his parents'
living room. Escape needs bribes. Even if the bank's open,
there might not be time for a withdrawal.

The cancer he had before I was born never recurred.
It could. Any day. Any hour. The polio he'd suffered
as a boy had left one leg thin. Since he insisted we live,
the three of us, in that one bedroom sardine can apartment,
what could Mother and I say?

He was always doing math on the backs of bills, old envelopes.
He was an artist of numbers:
One—starving stick
Two—poor peddler's pack
Three—beggar's hands
            cupped sideways
Four—the hardbacked chair
            turned upside down
Five—the bloated stomach

Why should Father go to doctors whose predictions he'd outlived
for twenty years? How could any of us know
the boils, the hunger for sweets, the thirst were signs?
One night he slipped into a diabetic coma,
the next day, he was dead.

After the funeral we found bank books, bonds,
those dollars we flipped through like a deck.
What were we supposed to do? Cry, scream,
beat our heads against the wall, giggle like hell,
our blouses soaked with tears.

LOIS ROSEN

Ethel Rosenberg and Me

i

June 1953

Cousin Richard had escaped his clothes
again, his tiny penis wiggling
as he ran through the lawn croquet.

But the grown-ups didn't blame him
this time when his mother fainted,
wise to be sick at broadcast news.

Down Faifie went, smoking Camel
still pinched between her sallow fingers.
Not commuted. Electrocuted.

Julius and Ethel. Voices crackled,
static on their GE radio
like heat lightning that June 13th.

I was in an off-the-shoulder blouse
and walking cast, sweat rolling between
newly plastered gauze and my shin.

ii

November 1953

On Thanksgiving that brat Richard died,
filled like turkey with salmonella,
a bolt no one but me, daughter

of card-carrying Commies, could fear
was caused by Ike, killer of two Reds.
Faifie, who'd had one breast removed,

soon followed Richard's small butterflied
corpse, the cancer spread to her brain.
I cried, lacking the grace to faint.

Leftists never mentioned Heaven;
all my parents said, as comfort, was
where they went, it's not the USA.

iii

December 1953

Knickerbocker Village at Chanukah,
creaky maroon-panelled elevators
smelled of chicken soup even on workdays.

The steam came up so fiercely that Grandma,
atheist matriarch, opened windows
to dusk's pigeons in the crumbling brickwork.

Potato-stuffed, I saw her finger point
to the brick building across the courtyard
where Ethel's mother was taking care of

Ethel's two darling boys, now she's gone.
I wondered which grandma would keep me
and my sister if my parents were jailed.

iv

March/April 1954

The buzz saw cracked my cast in March,
my calf emerging thin and wasted,
the light leg flying up at each step

like a Purim clown. I limped on.
My first blood flowed that Passover,
mark drawn by the Angel of Death

on my gateway. Stained, I came of age
with Queen Ethel, family image
of womanhood, condemned to the chair.

Wired as I was, she lived in me,
waiting for the next jolt. Not holding
haggadahs, we crossed our red seas.

JUDITH WERNER

Shoplifter Hands

The ego's reach is so strong
that yesterday, when I thought
I was wise, even
in the beautiful fall
Camassia Wildlife Refuge
where I'd gone in reverence
for all that remains of the wild,
for all that still
exists of peace,
I watched my two hands

merging fast as cars onto a freeway,
coming together in a concrete motion
to lift a bird's nest
away from the chosen branches
as if it were only a trinket in the mall,

as if emptiness could not be
refilled next spring. A quiet trill
pulled me over to the other side of desire.
I lowered my arms, swayed
in the quickening wind.

Diane Lillian Averill

Ghost Story

Diana Ma

Nora kicks over a full ashtray on the floor of her apartment and briefly considers cleaning the mess but instead stuffs a pack of cigarettes in the pocket of her jacket and leaves the apartment. She has not slept in three nights. Her thin shoes slip a little on the wet pavement, and a light drizzle dampens her face. Her walk is aimless, taking her past closed stores and traffic lights, and she finally takes refuge from the increasing rain under a covered bus stop. She doesn't notice at first that there is someone else at the stop. For a moment, there is only a collection of shadows at one end of the bench, but when she blinks, there is a man in a black overcoat.

"May I have a light?" he asks.

She hands him her lighter, notices that he doesn't have a cigarette, and hands him one of hers as well.

He lights the cigarette but keeps the lighter flame burning. In the illumination of the flame, Nora sees his face clearly for the first time—an attractive Asian face graced with black eyes, even blacker hair curving around smooth cheeks, and an open expression.

"Do you believe that when a flame turns green, a being from the ghost world has come into this one?" He lets the flame go out.

"Don't you mean blue?"

"You're right. In America, it is blue. In China, it is believed that the flame must turn green."

She is embarrassed that she did not know this difference.

He says, "There doesn't seem to be much difference between a blue or green flame. Then again, there doesn't seem to be much difference between the ghost and human world either. You just have to know, I suppose."

She notices that he has not smoked his cigarette and wonders if the request for a light was only a way of setting up a pass at her. He is looking at the rain though and doesn't seem interested in picking her up. Nora begins to wish that he *had* been trying to interest her with his line about ghosts.

"The rain seems to be slowing." He stands. "I will see you again." His smile is one of happy anticipation. He must be at least thirty, but the smile makes him look like a child.

Nora watches him walk through the rain, her interest piqued by his mixture of mystery and sweetness.

When she returns to her apartment in the early hours of the morning, she finally falls asleep on her couch and dreams of children ringing her with their arms, dancing around her. They are chanting that "ring-around-a-rosy" song, and then they all fall down, but it is not a playful fall. They simply collapse, their bodies motionless on a cement playground with limbs splayed in unnatural angles. She wakes up shaking from the nightmare and reaches out for her clock, turning it around so that she can see the digital numbers. Two hours. She has only slept for two hours. Briefly, she contemplates trying to go back to sleep—after all, it's not as if she has to go to work.

Nora had quit her job as a counselor two weeks ago. It seems inconceivable that she once thought she could be a counselor. And kids! Why kids? Lately, they had all looked like her sister. Sandra was twenty-four when she died last year, and even though these kids were a lot younger, they all looked exactly like her. Same set mouth, same closed eyes. Nora hadn't been able to help her either. A friend of Sandra's had said at the funeral, "When I look at you, I see Sandra. You look so much like her." The funny thing is that they had never looked alike growing up. Sandra wasn't even her real sister. The two of them had been adopted by their white parents from a Chinese orphanage. When did Nora get her mouth and eyes? When Sandra took those sleeping pills? All Nora knows is that when Sandra died, her grief pulled her out of the world she thought she wanted, and now she feels as lost as the children she used to counsel, as lost as her dead sister.

A few days later, Nora opens the closet door in her bedroom. A knee-high cardboard box sits alone; all the junk that used to be crammed into the closet has been cleared away to make room for the box. Carefully, she lifts the box and carries it to the living room where she sets it on the coffee table. She sits down on the couch and contemplates the box. Sandra's roommate had sent over some things she thought Nora would want, a full year ago, and Nora has not yet been able to open the box. She reaches out and touches the sealed surface; an edge of brown packing tape crinkles slightly in her fingers. What is she expecting to find in the box? Something to explain all the mystery of her sister? There seemed to be no reason for her sister's suicide. Sandra had friends and family. Their parents had loved them.

True, there was probably a lot Nora had not known about her sister. Whatever her problems had been, she had not turned to her family for help. Why hadn't Sandra been able to talk to her own sister? She and Sandra were close as young girls, but they had been drifting apart for years. Nora remembers the day Sandra returned from her first year at college. Nora had just received her graduate degree and was also home for vacation. One day, they got into an argument. Sandra was curled up in her bed and suddenly said that their parents had had no right to adopt them.

Nora was shocked. "What do you mean? We would have ended up in a Chinese orphanage all our lives or out on the streets. We're the lucky ones."

"That's what everyone says. Mom and Dad. Their friends. Our friends. Everyone. Now you. Aren't we grateful that Mom and Dad couldn't have children and decided to adopt two Chinese girls so that we'd have a better life in America?"

"What's gotten into you? You know our Chinese parents abandoned us. Mom and Dad rescued us."

"Stop it!" Sandra screamed. "I don't feel lucky. And I'm ungrateful, okay? I don't appreciate being rescued. I don't appreciate this life I've been given. If you do, that's great. It's great that you have a graduate degree and are dating a lawyer. If you're happy not knowing a single Chinese person besides me, then I'm happy for you." She curled up on her bed again and refused to talk to Nora any more. Later, she dropped out of school and had only sporadic contact with both parents and sister.

Nora bends down to the box, hooks a finger under the edge of the taped flap and tugs gently. Nothing gives. After a few more minutes of contemplation, she replaces the box in her closet.

The phone rings and it is her mother on the line. "Darling, where have you been?"

Nora feels guilty for not returning her messages over the last few days, especially since she knows her mother is more anxious about her after Sandra's death last year.

"Sorry, Mom." There is an awkward moment while Nora thinks of something more to say, but her mother beats her to it.

"Your father and I are thinking of coming to Seattle to visit you."

Nora hasn't seen her parents since Sandra's funeral, and she isn't sure what she feels. She wants to see them, but she is afraid. For years, she never believed Sandra really thought that their parents had no right to adopt them. Only after her death did Nora realize that she was serious, and this is the knowledge with which she cannot face her parents.

Nora is writing in her journal on a warm afternoon in the park when a shadow falls over her. It is the man she met at the bus stop two weeks ago, and he is holding her lighter out to her with an abashed smile.

"I forgot to give this back to you, but I said I'd see you again, didn't I?"

She returns his smile and takes the lighter. "Thank you. Please sit down."

When he sits next to her, she says, "I'm Nora."

"And I am Jesse."

"Nice to see you again, Jesse." She decides the name fits him—man/boy that he seems to be. "So, Jesse, have you been following me or is it just my luck that you found me?" She is being flirtatious, and it surprises her how long it has been since she has done this.

He falls in with her flirtation easily. "Oh, I picked you out and have been following you for years."

She laughs. "In that case, the least I can do is invite you to lunch."

Nora has a good time with him at lunch although they talk about nothing substantial. He tells her ghost stories that he has made up, in a fake ghostly voice that has her laughing instead of frightened.

"One more," he says finally. He speaks in his normal voice for this story. "There was a young girl who became pregnant. All day long, she worked and sang with her mind on her belly growing round as the moon, imagining how the child's limbs would fit softly in her arms. She imagined the wrinkled skin, the hair faint like shadows, the beauty of her warm child. So full of love was she for her child that she went to her birthing bed without fear, although this was long ago, a dangerous era for a woman to birth a child. When it was time for this woman to give birth, blood streamed like a red river from her body, and the midwife could not stop the bleeding. Then the woman screamed and screamed, as much from the fear of losing her baby as from the pain. The child was stillborn, and the heartbroken woman begged to hold her dead child, but before she could feel the baby in her arms, she too slipped away on that river of blood and died. Her sorrow made her a ghost. In the centuries since her death, she steals other people's children because she is searching for her own."

"What happens to the children then?"

"The story doesn't say."

"Isn't it your story though? Can't you make up an ending?"

His eyes drop. "That's not a story I made up. It's an old story." He is quiet, then says finally, "The children don't really belong to the realm of the dead. They're not human anymore either. I suppose they would become ghosts in between two worlds."

Nora doesn't say anything. The brief happiness she felt in his presence has fled and she feels the familiar dissatisfied feeling of the last few weeks returning.

"I would change the ending if I could," he says.

Nora nods. She knows he would.

Nora has agreed to meet Jesse the next day. He is waiting for her in the same spot they had met yesterday. He greets her with an exuberant smile and then points toward the sky. "Do you want to do that?"

She looks in the direction he is pointing. "Fly kites?" His enthusiasm is contagious, so she answers, "Sure! There's a kite shop across the street. Come on." She takes his hand and is amazed at the naturalness of the gesture. It is perhaps the first time since Sandra's death that she has been able to reach out to another person's touch without feeling self-conscious about physical intimacy.

At the kite shop, they survey their choices. At first, Jesse falls passionately in love with a yellow kite with a bright orange sun drawn on the fabric but then is seduced by a blue kite shaped like a fish. Nora laughs and points out her favorites, amused by how quickly Jesse agrees with her choices. Eventually, they choose the blue fish kite.

Nora hasn't flown a kite in years, and Jesse admits that this is his first kite-flying experiment. She and Jesse take turns running and shouting suggestions at each other in their attempts to get the kite airborne, but it flops down each time. Perhaps they are having too much fun to seriously try. At last, they simply walk; Jesse carries the bedraggled kite in his arms.

"Want to hear another ghost story?" Jesse asks.

Nora nods and waits in anticipation.

"Once, there was a village where a rich man lived. This man did just enough for his fellow villagers to avoid being seen as miserly but no more than that. He lived alone and had no family. One night, the sound of crying woke him from his sleep. He started up from his bed and stared all around but saw nothing. After a few minutes of the incessant wailing, he gathered enough courage to light a lantern and shine the light into the dim corners. Seeing nothing but cobwebs, he then checked his entire house, and the crying followed him as if it were right behind him, but still, he saw nothing. He dared not return to bed, so, in terror, he sat upright in a hard chair, clutching the lantern. Nothing harmed him, and as morning came, the sound of crying faded and disappeared altogether with the rising sun.

"Exhausted from his sleepless night, the man ran to his neighbor's house and knocked on the door. The woman of the house opened the door and looked over her neighbor who was wild-eyed and trembling.

" 'You look like you've seen a ghost,' she said.

" 'I think I've heard one!' he gasped. 'There was such crying all night in my house—I couldn't sleep!'

"The woman nodded. 'A child of the village died last night. It would be that child's ghost in your house.'

" 'But what am I to do?'

" 'Try burning paper money to appease the deceased spirit,' she suggested. She was already turning back to her household concerns, thinking about her own children and her husband to feed.

"The rich man asked, 'What would a child ghost want with money?' but the woman had already closed the door.

"Nonetheless, when the crying started in the middle of the next night, the man climbed hurriedly out of his bed and burned fake money with shaking fingers. He lit sheet after sheet of the brightly colored paper . . . and still the crying did not cease.

"The next morning, the man was back at his neighbor's house, pounding frantically at the door. She answered the door with a baby at her hip and another child pulling at the hem of her skirt. 'Oh, it's you again,' she said with some impatience, but when she saw his paleness and even more pronounced trembling, she relented. 'It didn't work, did it?'

" 'No!' he wailed.

"'Why don't you try burning some cinnabar? That got rid of a ghost my aunt had haunting her.'

"'What if that doesn't work?'

"From inside the house, a child yelled, 'Mom, the rice porridge is burning!'

"'Then stir it!' she called back to her child, but she was already moving back into the house. 'Try the cinnabar!' she said to the man over her shoulder.

"The rich man trudged dejectedly away from his neighbor's house with little confidence that this new scheme would work, but he went to the market and bought large quantities of cinnabar. That night, as the crying began, the man burned the cinnabar and sent great clouds of red smoke into the rafters, but the crying continued. The noise scraped up and down his spine, and finally, he gave up burning cinnabar and simply moaned along with the ghost until morning.

"This time, the woman opened the door before he knocked. She had had a slight attack of conscience over her previous brusqueness and had been watching for him out of her window. 'Well, I don't have to ask if it worked,' she said before he could say anything. 'I've been thinking over your problem and think we've been going about it the wrong way. Paper money is to placate ghosts who have been wronged, and I don't suppose the ghost of a child would be after you for a wrong you did to it. Cinnabar repels malicious ghosts, and I don't believe yours means any harm. It's probably just lonely and scared.'

"'What am I supposed to do about that?' he snapped, his short temper the result of two frightening and sleepless nights.

"She didn't take offense though; she simply replied, 'I think you need to treat the ghost as if it were a real child. Give it enough care so that it will be strong enough to leave your house and roam the world.'

"'What kind of care?'

"'Oh, food. Clothes. That sort of stuff. One more thing—it would help if you would talk a bit to it.'

"'I'm too scared to talk to it!'

"'You want it to leave you alone, don't you?' Having done her neighborly duty, she went back into her house.

"By nightfall, the man had finished his preparations. At the first sound of crying, he sternly told himself to remain calm, but he was still nervous as he set out a bowl of goat's milk. He was disconcerted when the milk was slowly drained from the bowl by the invisible ghost, but he realized that the crying had stopped and he felt relief. However, his relief was short-lived. When the bowl was empty, the crying resumed. Hastily, the man set out a tailored set of child's clothing, commissioned just that day at great cost, and warm child's blankets, but the ghost continued crying. The man understood then that he had no choice but to try to comfort the child by talking to it. He stumbled and stuttered through awkward words of comfort, and the crying again ceased. He found that he had to keep talking or else the ghost would wail even louder. Gradually, his voice grew smoother, and his nerves became soothed by the sound of his own voice telling half-forgotten bedtime stories. A lullaby tugged at his memory, and he tenderly sang it to the ghost child. When he finished the song, his throat was too hoarse to continue talking. He waited for the sound of crying, but there was only silence. Outside it was still night. For another hour he stayed awake, listening for the ghost child, but it seemed that the ghost was truly gone. Worn out, he lay down in his bed and slept at last.

"The man was weeding his garden the next morning when his neighbor came over to lean on his fence. She had been a bit curious to see what had happened with the ghost and decided to stop at his house.

"'Is it gone?' she asked.

"'It's gone,' he said but then added, 'I don't understand it though. Why did it come to me?'

"'You have a big house with hardly anyone in it. Maybe it just looked for a house empty enough for it to inhabit and heal from being torn from the living.'

"'Maybe so. I wonder where it will go now? What will happen to it?'

"The woman shrugged, her curiosity already satisfied. 'At least it's gone.'

"The man was strangely uncomfortable with her answer. He could not help but feel some concern for a ghost child on its own in the world. Perhaps if he had made a sincere welcome, the ghost would have stayed longer. He regretted its leaving a little. But only a little."

When Jesse finishes the story, Nora isn't sure what to think. They had been walking slowly up a hill while he was telling the story, and she stops now to catch her breath. The story seems too strange and moving to be a typical scary and gory ghost story. "Thank you," she says at last, as if he has given her a present.

"You're welcome," he replies. Then, suddenly, he flings the kite into the air and runs down the hill. Nora's heart lightens when he flashes her a triumphant grin. The kite rises into the sky and soars. It soars as if nothing could ever bring it down.

"So, who is this new guy you're seeing?" Robert, her lawyer ex-boyfriend, asks.

Nora and Robert are having one of their infrequent get-togethers at a downtown restaurant. She answers Robert with something vague, but he persists in asking questions about where Jesse lives, what he does for a living, if he has family—questions to which she doesn't have answers. Nora has to admit that Jesse's lack of history *does* puzzle her, but she knows that if she asks Jesse, he will tell her something completely plausible, and it will not be until later that she again feels uneasy about how little she really knows about him. Finally, she tells Robert, "I like him. Can't we leave it at that?"

"Fine. Just be careful."

"You and I were both such careful people with each other. Coasters for our glasses, balanced checkbooks every month, and two different kinds of birth control. Life's not like that."

Robert nods. "You're right. We were getting in a rut. But this Jesse—this is different?"

She laughs. "This is a man who tells me a new ghost story almost every day. Different is an understatement."

When Nora gets home, the conversation with Robert is still on her mind and makes her really think about the relationship with Jesse. She wants badly to talk to Jesse but doesn't even have his phone number. He always calls her or stops by her apartment, so she has never needed a way to reach him before. She thinks of him showing up at her apartment unexpectedly or waiting for her after work, excited about whatever new thing they are going to do that day. He never wants to repeat an outing. If they fly a kite one day, he wants to go to a concert next, but he is always, inevitably, joyous.

"Nora."

She jumps and spins around to find Jesse standing inside the door. "How did you get in here? I didn't even hear you come in!" She must have left the door open when she got back to the apartment.

He looks discomfited and asks, "Is this a bad time? I could come back later."

"No, I want to talk to you."

He catches her up in his arms and kisses her. "I missed you." He says it again, in Chinese.

She repeats it, laughing at how strange it sounds coming from her. "Did I get it right?"

"You're close. Try again." He is patient with her, repeating words over and over again. "What else do you want to learn?" he asks when she is finally able to tell him she misses him in Chinese and make him smile.

"Say my name."

"It doesn't translate. You'll have to choose a new name if you want a Chinese one."

She leans her head against his shoulder. "Do you have a phone number? I don't even know how to reach you when I want to ask you to help me choose a name."

"I don't have a phone." He pauses. "Nora?"

"Yes?"

"I wish I could give you more. You've given me so much happiness."

She is surprised. "What do you mean? I've been just as happy with you."

"I know, but sometimes, when you think I am asleep or reading a book, you look as sad as you did when I first met you at the bus stop. I want to do something to help."

"You teach me Chinese. Even Sandra never tried that."

"That's what I mean. You don't talk about your sister except to say that she is dead."

"I'm confused about my sister." She shakes her head. "I don't think anyone could understand." She feels strangely compelled to try to explain Sandra to him. "Do you remember that ghost story you told me? The one about the stolen children who grow up between the world of the dead and the human world? That's how Sandra always felt. She felt she couldn't get balanced between a Chinese world she'd lost and a white world she couldn't fit into. I was better at believing I fit in . . . until she died. She was my anchor. Even if I couldn't admit I felt the displacement of our lives as much as she did, I needed her." Nora can feel her throat clench and tears slide down her face. "I was scared of what she believed and couldn't reach out to her. Now that she's dead, I've inherited all her confusion."

Jesse holds her tightly. "I understand. It is not easy, but you are strong. You will find a way to live with what your sister understood, without her sorrow."

Nora wishes she were so sure. "You have a child's optimism. Not that the children I worked with ever had your optimism. You are more like a healed child—one I've always hoped to see."

"Then you have healed me."

She laughs without humor. "You'd be the first. There's nothing that I can heal."

"No, you're wrong." He kisses her so that she cannot think of asking him any more questions.

Nora faces her parents in her living room. Her mother is asking how she feels about their decision to remodel Sandra's old bedroom.

"I just can't bear to have it the way it is," she is saying. "She was a happy child. And then she was just gone. When she left school, I was afraid she would get mixed up with the wrong crowd."

Only her mother could say something like "wrong crowd." She has a way of using outdated sayings that go along with her old-fashioned ideas. She had disapproved of one of Sandra's boyfriends just because he had long hair.

Nora nods and says, "Go ahead and remodel the room. I don't mind." Actually, she never remembered Sandra as a particularly happy child, but she isn't about to say that to her mother. About a year before she died, Nora had asked Sandra why she wouldn't visit their parents. Sandra had surprised her, saying that she didn't want to hurt them. Nora knows what she means now. Their parents wouldn't have known what to do about Sandra's resentment and confusion. Nora wished she had just once told her sister, "You're not wrong to feel confused. I feel the same way."

"How is Robert?" her mother asks, trying to sound casual.

"Martha, don't start," her father counsels.

Nora breaks into the familiar bantering. "I'm dating someone. He's Chinese. Last night, we were choosing a name for me in Chinese." She wants to know what they will think about Jesse.

"You want to change your name?" her father asks doubtfully. "Like Sandra? She wanted to change her name. I never could understand."

"It was those hippies she was friends with. Her name meant something like gold lily," her mother added.

"Mom, Chinese names have meanings like 'gold lily.' It wasn't a 'hippie' thing."

"Oh really?" Her mother's voice is over-bright, the way Nora knows it is when she is trying to disguise her discomfort.

"Listen, I'm not changing my name." Nora gives up her struggle to explain what it means to her to finally learn a few Chinese words.

"I'm sorry, dear," her mother apologizes. "You were telling us about the new man in your life."

Nora begins to regret bringing up Jesse. "He's not really in my life. He's just someone I started seeing."

Her mother nods. "You seem happier lately. Maybe it's because you're seeing someone. This last year has been hard on you, I know." She glances at her husband. "We were worried. We wanted to come earlier, but you were always so busy. If anything is ever wrong, you tell us." Her voice breaks. "We just wanted you girls to be happy. We loved you both so much."

"I know. I know that." Nora wants to reassure her mother that their love is enough. It is what she has tried to believe all her life, and she is sure that Sandra wanted to believe that as well. Every time a kid taunted them at school, she and Sandra ran to their parents for their love, but neither girl ever said a word about their playground trials. Nora, as the older sister, used to fight anyone who would pick on her and Sandra, the only Chinese girls in their mostly white suburban school, but when her parents scolded her, she could never explain what had happened. Eventually, Nora stopped fighting other children, and Sandra had stopped sobbing in her mother's lap with her nameless pain. Neither anger nor love had been able to heal them.

Jesse is pacing Nora's small living room, seeming unusually agitated. "I can't stay for much longer," he says finally.

She is sitting on the couch, waiting for him to tell her what is wrong. "You can't stay the night?"

"That's not what I mean. I have to go away for good. Soon. I don't know how long I have with you."

Her stomach turns cold. "What are you talking about? You live somewhere else?"

"Yes."

"Well." She rises from the couch. "Why didn't you tell me before?"

He looks at her helplessly. "It's complicated."

"What is this then? Just a fling?" She is getting angrier. "I suppose it's also going to be too complicated to see you again. You could have told me that you were leaving town!"

Jesse begins to move toward her but then seems to change his mind when she glares at him. "I thought I had more time. You seemed so sad when I first saw you. Like me. I thought we could help each other."

"You never seemed sad."

"I'm not. Not any more." He smiles at her, and though it is graver than his usual delighted, uncomplicated smile, it still stops her heart. "Thank you, Nora."

This time he does move toward her, and she doesn't push him away when he draws her to his body.

"Why are you leaving?"

"I would have to be sad to stay, and I am growing so light that I will float away soon. Ghosts do that. They flicker in with a green—or blue—flame, and then they leave when they aren't bound to this world by sorrow."

"But you're not a ghost!"

"Break my heart," he suggests, "so that I will stay in your world out of sorrow and haunt your bed at night. You won't even know I am there, and I will watch you forever when you sleep—"

"Don't! Don't joke!" she cries. "Our lives are not some ghost story you made up!"

He looks down at his feet. "I can't help what I am."

"Who are you, anyway?" she asks heatedly. "You've never even told me anything about yourself!"

"I have told you everything about my life."

"You've told me nothing but ghost stories!"

He is silent. The most impossible possibility gains shape in his silence.

"No. Oh no," she whispers.

"Nora, I've been telling you stories about my life all along. I told you the story of how I lost my soul. It was stolen. And then you gave it back to me. And now I have to leave."

Nora thinks of the things she has never been able to understand. How he appears silently at her apartment door, how he has no history and numerous uncertainties about human life. "You're serious." Her voice is flattened of all emotion, and she needs to sit down on the couch.

"I'm sorry."

"Sorry. You tell me that you're a ghost and that you have to leave, and you're sorry!" Shock makes her voice rise.

"I'm more than sorry." Jesse sits next to her on the couch. "Nora, I do almost want you to weigh me down with sorrow so that I can stay with you. Is that what you want?"

The thought of hurting him, binding a grieving presence forever, appalls her. She cannot wish to hold him at such a high price. She may have failed to help her sister, but she will not fail Jesse, another stolen child. "No. That is not what I want. I want to take away all your sorrow so that you will be free to leave." She touches his arm, timidly, realizing with a kind of disbelief that she is touching someone not quite alive. "I will just miss you."

"You'll survive in this world. I know you will."

"That is the shortest story you have ever told me. You have to do better than that."

He tells her stories into the night, and every one is beautiful, and every one has ghosts. She cries at the end of each one.

Nora pries one end of the tape loose from the cardboard and peels open Sandra's box. She lifts out each item with care, her hands trembling. A silver necklace with a jade pendant that Sandra used to wear all the time. An anthology of poems that Nora had inscribed with a birthday greeting on the inside cover. A blue flannel throw blanket, the twin of one Nora also has because their mother had worried about the two of them getting cold in the winters of strange cities. An old shirt of their father's that Sandra had "borrowed" years ago and never returned. Sandra's adoption certificate. A framed picture of the family—two Chinese girls at ages six and ten grinning madly at the camera while their two white parents each held a daughter tenderly in their arms.

Nora stares at the last item for a long time. She had not been wrong to remember Sandra as a sad child, but apparently neither had her mother been wrong to remember Sandra as happy. She remembers the day the picture was taken, even though at the time it had just seemed to be a silly day of running in the backyard and playing mud-splattered games with Sandra. Their parents had been content to watch them all afternoon from the porch and even serve as props for their games when needed. Somehow, watching their daughters play so wildly and joyously had seemed to drive concerns about muddy children's clothes and household tasks from their parents' minds. That day, they had been the kind of family that someone, a neighbor perhaps, had wanted to record with a picture. Strange that Nora had forgotten the simple fact of her sister ever being happy.

One by one, she picks up the other objects and lines them up in a row. She is touched that Sandra had kept her family's presents and keepsakes so that after her death, her roommate could gather them up and send them to Nora for comfort. There are, after all, no answers among her sister's things, no easy explanation for her depression. It is perhaps enough for Nora to believe that her sister had loved them all . . . even though she had left them.

"That's not going to work," Jesse says, coming up behind her.

Nora has just finished lighting the last candle and blows out the match. "What are you talking about? I'm just lighting candles." Silently, they survey her apartment covered with dozens of tall lit candles, burning so hot that the flames are tinged blue . . . or perhaps green.

"I will be gone tonight."

"So soon." She speaks flatly, not inviting an answer.

Nora pulls off his shirt and then hers so that their skin can touch. "See. You are as real as I am." She kisses him, proving to them both that the heat of his body is real. There is the feather brush of his fingers against her spine. His breath warm against her mouth. The hard contours of his body pressed against her. They are flesh against flesh. She hears his cry of release, and then there is nothing but air against her heated skin.

DIANA MA

RAINBOWS AND ROSES

ELAINE WINER

I'm sitting on the balcony watching the ocean one night about ten, thinking about taking one of those yellow pills the doctor gave me for depression, when there's a knock at the door. I'm no spring chicken, and it's an effort for me to get up from the chair. While I'm struggling, there's another knock, then a whole series of poundings and tappings. I come inside from the balcony and limp across the living room muttering, "I'm coming, I'm coming." You try moving around fast at sixty with bad knees.

I open the door. The hall's dimly lit, and I can't see clearly at first. Then I see Nonnie.

I stagger and grab the door frame, trying to gulp air into my lungs. I must still be sleeping on the patio and dreaming that I'm answering the door. How else could I see Nonnie? I went to visit her grave at Mt. Sinai after work yesterday, just like I do every Wednesday.

"I'm so glad to get home, Ellie," Nonnie says, pushing by me and hobbling into the living room. Her words come breathless and fast, as they always do when she's excited or upset. "If you'd been out I don't know what I would have done. I must have fallen asleep or something, and when I opened my eyes I was walking down Ocean Drive in South Beach! I had no idea how I'd gotten there. I didn't have my purse, so I promised the cabbie I'd pay when I got home."

I follow her into the living room where she throws herself on the couch. My legs are so weak I sink down next to her, then I jump up and stand by the door. My knees are shaking so hard I lean on the back of a chair. I can't talk.

"He's waiting, Ellie," Nonnie says after a minute. I just look at her, my mouth open. She says again, with that little edge her voice gets when she's impatient, "Ellie, the cab driver is waiting downstairs to get paid."

I grab my purse and race down the elevator to the front of the condo. Sure enough, there's a taxi there, and an ancient little man in the driver's seat.

"I picked up that little crippled lady and brought her here even when she said she'd lost her purse and didn't have any money," he says. I give him ten dollars, and he eyes it sadly. "I could have left her down on South

Beach. I could have had plenty of fares who didn't tell me how fast to drive and say, 'Watch, you're going to hit the curb.'" I put another dollar in his hand, then run back upstairs.

Nonnie's in the kitchen.

"Where are my snacks?" she asks, her head in the refrigerator. "You don't have anything good in here, and I'm starving. What happened to my rice custards and my blueberry muffins?"

I always kept a lot of soft snacks for Nonnie. She's had rheumatoid arthritis for forty years and, once it spread to her jaw, she had trouble chewing. She is—was—disabled (I can't get my tenses straight). I guess some people would call her crippled or deformed, but my little sister's actually very beautiful. She has great big green eyes and long lashes she's always batting around and the sweetest mouth. What makes her so cute is that she's so little, and yet she's absolutely fearless. I guess Mom and I loved her so much all her life she felt safe and never realized how she looked to other people.

She and I never argued and fought like other sisters. I always cared for her as if I were a second mother, while she was always picking on me and acting smart, but in a cute way. People said we were like the Odd Couple on television.

"Sylvie cleaned out the refrigerator," I say. My voice is squeaky, but at least it's coming back. I don't add that since she and Mom died, the only one I've let into the apartment has been Sylvie, the cleaning woman, and she threw Nonnie's snacks out over twelve months ago.

I make Nonnie scrambled eggs and white bread, heaping on the butter. She calms down a little as she eats, but she's still upset.

"How could Sylvie throw away my snacks?" she asks. When she finishes eating, she says, "I can't wait to get into a hot shower. I don't know why I feel so dirty." I have a sudden vision of her body lying under the earth at Mt. Sinai Cemetery. I close my eyes tight for a moment, then I say, "Come into the bathroom and I'll help you shower."

As we walk down the hall I'm thinking—*who am I really putting in my shower?* I look at her feet to see if they're turned backward. Nonnie once told me that's a sign of the walking dead. Her feet are frontward, and she's wearing her orthopedic shoes.

I help her undress. She can do it herself, but it takes her forever because she has to use her handicapped stick with a hook on one end to get her blouse over her head. I adjust the shower head so the spray won't be too hard, then turn on the shower.

Her body looks just the way it did before she died—thin, wasted almost, her neck set at an odd angle because the bones of her shoulders are almost gone. Her breasts are still full and beautiful. They bring tears to my eyes, set upon that ruin of a body. I soap a washcloth and rub her arms and legs lightly, then wash the rest of her. There are no private parts when you're crippled. I'm satisfied after that shower that, dead or not, she's nice and clean. No mold, no graveyard smell. I finish by shampooing her hair.

"It was so awful, Ellie. I don't know what happened to me," she says, closing her eyes while I wash out the conditioner. "All I can remember is darkness, then opening my eyes and there I am walking down Ocean Drive in South Beach. I knew where I was immediately because I saw Cafe New. I went in and asked for Michael, and he came out of the kitchen and helped me get the cab."

When Mom, Nonnie, and I wanted a big night out, we'd eat at Cafe New in South Beach. The food was good, and Michael would always sit down at our table and joke and talk for a few minutes. That means a lot to three bachelor ladies. Michael's not only a nice man, but he's handsome too.

Although neither of us had married, Nonnie's always been a great admirer of handsome men. Just before she died, she'd put an ad in the singles column of the *Miami Herald: "Red-haired married woman in her late teens looking for companion for wild fun."* Reading the answers kept her happy for days.

As I towel-dry Nonnie, it occurs to me I should tell her what's really going on. We never hid secrets from each other before. I open my mouth to tell her she's dead, but this isn't something you can just blurt out cold. The timing has to be right.

"Is it too late to watch *Gilligan's Island?*" Nonnie asks, coming out of her bedroom. She smells from her talcum, a nice floral scent, and looks fresh and clean as a little kid.

"You look tired. Better go to bed early tonight," I say. It's easier than telling her the reruns are off the tubes.

"I'll just say good night to Mom." She pushes past me and goes as fast as she can down the hall toward Mom's room, but I'm faster. I get in front of her and stand with my back to the door.

She'll never be able to sleep if she sees I've turned Mom's room into a study. What could be more terrifying than opening your eyes to find yourself walking down Ocean Drive without knowing how you got there, and when you get home your sister tells you that you've died? And to top it off, your mother's dead too? I can't do that to her at night. I promise myself I'll tell her tomorrow at the latest.

"You have amnesia for sure," I tell her. "You know perfectly well Mom went to visit Judy in New Jersey for a few weeks." Judy's our oldest sister, the one who married and moved away.

"I don't remember Mom going to visit Judy," Nonnie says, looking troubled. "I can't believe I'd forget that. Are you sure Mom's all right?"

I put her to bed, then get into bed myself, but I can't sleep. I twist and turn, my blanket on the floor, the pillow over my head. I have to tell Nonnie about her and Mom being dead and I know it'll make her feel awful. Maybe I can wait and we can be happy like we were before. Just for a little time.

My head hurts so I go into the bathroom and take three aspirins. Instead of getting back into bed, I lean out the window of my bedroom. It's started to rain, the soft gray rain of Florida. I'd forgotten the smell of gray Florida rain. By the time I pull my head back in, my hair is soaked.

I've realized something. It was so awful losing the only two people in the world that I loved, that this past year I was kind of dying inside. I was pulling away from a world that had given me so much pain. I didn't want to feel anything anymore, ever.

In the morning, Nonnie's sitting up in bed looking happy and rested. I'd given her hair a red rinse just before she died, and the sun lights it up into a neon-red halo. I hug her hard, and then I hug her again.

"What a commotion! You'd think I was gone a year," she says, grinning. "Ellie, let's have breakfast in South Beach."

"Why?" I ask.

"I don't know. I just feel like celebrating. Let's go to Cafe New!"

"But you were just there yesterday," I say. "We don't go to South Beach twice in one week."

But all the time I'm getting dressed up to go to South Beach. I don't know why I always have to say *no* first. I hate that in myself. "I don't think we should go," I say.

We're halfway to South Beach when we pass our favorite bakery. Nonnie asks me to stop and pick up blueberry muffins. I go in and Mrs. Gonzales asks me, "How's your sister?" "Fine," I say. "Well, have a wonderful holiday," she says. I get back into the car. Nonnie opens the bag, and then and there we eat four of the muffins. I lick the crumbs and butter off my fingers, then put my head down on the wheel and start to cry. I really cry up a storm, I can't believe how much I'd missed blueberry muffins. Nonnie pats me and murmurs, "There, there."

Finally I reach over and give Nonnie's cheek a kiss.

"What's that for?" she asks, pert as a Pekinese. She wipes the butter off her cheek. "All this hugging and kissing!"

"I'd forgotten how good they taste," I say. "The muffin and the kiss both."

She fixes me with a heavily meaningful look. "Let's hope Sylvia doesn't disappear these from the refrigerator too."

We park on Eighth and Ocean and cross the grass to the wide concrete promenade that runs along the beach. We pass the place where they rent roller skates.

"Let's try it, Ellie!" Nonnie says. "I used to skate as a kid, before I got sick. It was so much fun."

"You're crippled and I'm sixty years old," I say. "I probably have osteoporosis and I'll break a leg for sure." But she keeps after me, and finally I rent two pairs of skates from the little store on the side of the walk.

I find an empty bench on the promenade and start putting on Nonnie's skates. The path is crowded, tourists and residents walking up and down, skaters and joggers darting between and around them. A young boy is carrying a radio, and Spanish music fills the warm, gusty air. On the beach, there's a volleyball game going on. Two teams of almost-naked youngsters are jumping and yelling, and I smell coconut oil and sweat.

Nonnie's skates fit fine, and so do mine, which is miraculous considering how much money the two of us spend on made-to-order shoes. I manage to stand up, then help Nonnie to her feet. We're vertical about four seconds, but then our legs go out from under us, and we're back on the bench again.

"This is crazy," I say. "We're in no condition to walk fast, let alone roller skate."

"Please let's try again," Nonnie begs.

So we stand up, clinging to each other like a couple of drunks, and start down the path taking small, scared steps. My left arm is around Nonnie's waist, my right waving around in front of me like I'm leading a band.

Suddenly my left foot touches down upon the rough concrete walk with a kind of *skritch*, a noise like two electric wires touching. I get a feeling of how hard that concrete really is, and I sense below the concrete the whole solid earth, the layers of rock, the fire at the center, the enormity of a planet turning in space, all beneath my left foot. And I know it's big enough to support one skinny old woman.

I put my whole weight on that skate and glide down the promenade on one foot like an octogenarian swan. It feels so good I lean forward and raise my right leg behind me. I even hold out the arm that isn't holding Nonnie, like I'm on the Olympic skating team. I pass a startled old man and give him a little wave. "Hi there," I yell. Then I put down my right leg and balance on that for a while.

Up until now I've been pulling Nonnie along with me, but as we start moving really fast I feel her skating too, moving her legs, swaying from side to side with me. Left, right. Left, right. The Spanish music lodges in our bright wheels, and we fly along in perfect rhythm, our hair lifting in the breeze, our cheeks and eyes bathed with cool, rushing air. I see the startled eyes of people, I see birds, helicopters, clouds, red jackets, and blue sky, all of it melting into streamers of holiday color that whirl by us. We're skating, we're skating, our lives flowing from one to the other through our joined hands, our legs pushing together in long, swooping trajectories. I look at Nonnie and I've never seen her look so beautiful, her cheeks the red of good health, her eyes glittering with excitement. I have a sense of moving above the world, above the planet.

"Rainbows and roses," Nonnie sings as we fly by faster and faster.

"And fuzzy white kittens," I sing with her as I always do. My Nonnie!

I'm taking off Nonnie's skates when I decide that this is the moment to tell her.

"There's something I have to tell you," I say. "You're dead, Nonnie."

"I'm not tired at all. You know, Ellie, I'll bet this is how you feel after you make love!"

I can't help smiling. For years we'd talked about how it might feel to have a man love you. Did it really leave you feeling like this, uplifted, full of certainty that life would turn out all right? That there was no death, no grave worms, no ceasing, no forever leave-taking?

But I get back to business. This is the right time to tell Nonnie, I feel it in my bones. But how am I going to make her believe me?

I get an idea. I'd taken her to Iris, a psychic on Collins Avenue, the week before she died. "Remember when we went to Iris for a reading, and she said you were going to acquire a small piece of real estate and settle down permanently in Florida?"

"I remember," she says.

"Well, you got the land," I say. "It was about six feet by three. Mother got hers too. It was a double funeral."

"You're trying to tell me something's happened to Mother?" she asks, going pale. "Is that how I got amnesia? Because something happened to her and I couldn't face it?" She begins to cry. "Oh Ellie, is she dead?"

"Well, yes," I say. "But that's not the worst."

"What could be worse than that?" she asks.

"I told you. You're dead too."

She looks at me, her eyes wide. After a moment, she touches my cheek and says, "Poor Ellie! You looked almost dead yourself yesterday, although you look a lot better now. You must have had a nervous breakdown after Mom died, the way I had amnesia."

"I can show you your grave," I say. "I've been there often enough. When they told us Mom died during the exploratory, you said 'I can't live without her' and dropped dead too. Even though it happened in the hospital they couldn't bring you back."

"I can't believe I'm dead," she says, but I see by her eyes she's beginning to remember. I put my arms around Nonnie and hold her until she stops shaking, the two of us sitting on the bench in the bright sunlight.

"Strange things are happening to us," I say. "I can't believe we just went roller-skating. You've been crippled since you were eighteen, and I never skated before."

"It was wonderful," Nonnie says. She really looks at me. "Poor Ellie! With Mother and me both gone, you must be pretty lonely."

"Maybe I'm dreaming you," I say, kissing her hand, wetting it with my tears. "Maybe I missed you so much that now I'm imagining you're here."

"That's sweet," Nonnie says, "but I'm definitely here. I feel no different than I did before—you know—I died. What on earth is happening to us?"

"We always told each other that whoever went first would try to contact the other. Maybe that's what this is."

"I'm really here, not in your mind. I'm back in the flesh. And I feel better than I have for a long time."

After a while we go across the street to Cafe New and order the special of the day, grilled chicken. We eat every bit of it and finish off with apple pie and vanilla ice cream.

"I don't know why I came back or what's going to happen tomorrow," Nonnie says, tilting her head to get the very last drop of cappuccino, "but right now I'm happy. Really happy." She lays her hand on my arm and her love flows through me like honey.

Don't ever forget this moment, I think, looking around me. South Beach and sunshine, the crowds hurrying along Ocean Drive, her hand on my arm. *Don't ever forget.*

We get home around seven and turn on the set and watch some of the new sitcoms that have come onto the tube since I stopped watching last year. I'd forgotten how much fun television is when there are two people laughing together on the couch and the night is safely shut out, the dark wind that blows across the high balcony shut out by the strong sliding door.

Around eleven, I help her into her nightgown. She climbs into bed and I fix her pillows, the hard one underneath, the soft one on top the way she likes them.

"It was a great day," she says when I lean down to kiss her. "I never thought in a million years I'd ever skate again."

When I get up in the morning, Nonnie's gone. I look all over the apartment two or three times. The fourth time I open the door to her bedroom closet, I pull aside the liner in the shower, I pull open the sliding doors and go out on the balcony, and for some reason I even open the refrigerator door, but Nonnie's not anywhere. I go to South Beach and search for her there, but all the time I know I'm not going to find her.

I go to Cafe New and sit at a sidewalk table. Michael comes over and sits down.

"I heard about your sister and mother," he says. "I'm sorry."

"They died a year ago," I say.

"I would have sent you a card, but I didn't know where you lived. You just stopped coming so I couldn't ask for your address."

"You didn't see us come in for lunch yesterday, my sister and me?"

"How could I have seen her yesterday if she's dead?" Michael gives me a look. "Are you all right? I guess holidays are hard when you've lost someone you love. I guess Christmas would be the time you'd miss them most of all." A tear rolls down his cheek. I remember he lost his lover from AIDS a few years before.

I look around and notice the lights strung over the palm trees and the red bows on the fire hydrants. I know suddenly that if I ask Romeros, the doorman at my condo, if he saw Nonnie come to the door in a taxi on Christmas Eve, he'd say she wasn't ever there.

"Nobody ever thinks that might be the time when the ones we've lost miss us the most too," I say. I kiss Michael's wet cheek. "I know Alex would love to come back and comfort you this Christmas. I'll bet he's thinking about you this very minute." Michael gives me a dazed, radiant look. "I'd better let you go," I say. "It was nice of you to sit down and talk when you're so busy. You're a nice man, Michael. Nonnie always liked you."

"She was a very special lady," he says. "Full of life, you know?" He leans down and kisses my cheek. "Thank you," he whispers, and goes back into the kitchen.

I finish my coffee, pay the bill, and walk across Ocean Drive toward the beach. The promenade isn't as crowded as it was yesterday when Nonnie and I went skating, maybe because the holiday is over.

I walk out onto the sand and take off my shoes. I'd forgotten how good warm sand feels underneath your feet. I'm not ready to go swimming, but it's such a beautiful day I don't think I'll go home yet either.

I walk down to the water and stand there looking out at the ocean. The wind lifts my hair, then pats it down again like a gentle hand. A wave comes rushing up, kisses my toes with rich, cold foam, then slides back into the ocean.

ELAINE WINER

TEETH

TAMARA MUSAFIA

The water was boiling. I took the *dzhezva,* Turkish coffeepot, off the stove, poured out some of the water, and put in three teaspoons of coffee. I put the *dzhezva* back on the stove and watched the dark brown cloud rise. I moved the coffee till it settled and put it back on the heat again.

"Three boils make good coffee," I said to Shpresa, my granddaughter, who was setting the table for breakfast.

"And when you roast the coffee beans, sprinkle them with sugar," she said, imitating my voice. "See, Nana, I know it all already."

She knows it all already. Only fourteen and she knows it all already.

"Halil, coffee is almost ready," I called to my husband, who was shaving in the bathroom.

I was waiting for the last boil when the door shook open. I turned to see two soldiers with machine guns enter the kitchen. Shpresa dropped the plate and moved behind me. The coffee boiled over and its pleasant aroma was overpowered by the biting, burning smell.

The soldiers wore black wool caps with holes for eyes and mouths.

"What are you waiting for?" the taller soldier yelled in Serbian.

Halil, still with shaving foam on his face, entered the kitchen behind the soldier. The soldier turned and pointed the gun at him. I saw the red tiger of Serbian paramilitary forces sewn on the sleeve of his camouflage uniform.

"You have five minutes to get out or we shoot!" he said.

I felt pain in my gut as if I had been hit with an iron fist. It was this pain and fear for my family that made me put on the black shoes, the gray raincoat, and the white scarf over my head. Shpresa put on her jeans jacket and her favorite red wool sweater over it. Halil and Ferid, my youngest son, followed our example and in less then five minutes we were at the door.

"Out!" the soldier yelled and out we went.

My Serbian neighbor, Zora, was crying at her doorstep. I wanted to say good-bye but the soldier turned to her and yelled, "What are you looking at! Get back, you stupid woman!"

She closed her door. Only two days ago she was telling me I should put a Serbian nameplate on the door. It would have been easy to change Albanian Berisha to Serbian Berishich, but Halil wouldn't hear of that.

Now it was happening. The horror stories we were hearing about from Pech had come to Prishtina, to Boro and Ramiz Street No. 15.

In the street, people were coming from adjacent apartment buildings in small groups of five to ten, each group with its own tormentors yelling at them. People in pajamas, in raincoats, carrying children, carrying plastic bags, umbrellas, suitcases, toys—all converged on the street and made a river of sorrow and despair.

"Dzevad, Dzeneta, Mehmet," a mother was calling her children.

"Come on, it will all be fine," a husband was comforting his crying wife.

"I knew this was going to happen," a woman was saying.

I walked slowly ahead in the morning mist, holding Shpresa's hand and praying silently for our lives. Halil and Ferid were walking in front of us.

When we arrived at the railroad station, there were thousands of people. It looked like half of the city was at the station. None of the faces looked familiar. Only the expression was familiar—no one knew why were we there on this cold April morning but we all knew that nothing good would happen to us.

Some said, "It's good they didn't take the men."

Some said, "NATO will bomb the station—that's why they brought us here."

Some said, "They are looting our homes this very moment."

Some said, "They'll kill us all!"

"Nana, what happens next?" Shpresa asked me.

I opened my raincoat and hugged her inside of it. "It will be OK," I said.

"I forgot my Walkman," she said.

"I left all the jewelry," I said. "And you know what else?"

"No," she answered and looked at me.

"I forgot my teeth," I said softly.

Shpresa started to laugh. She threw her head back and showed all her perfect white teeth. Her black eyes filled with tears as she laughed.

"What's with you, Shpresa?" Ferid asked.

"Nana forgot her teeth," she answered and pointed at me. I turned away from them and covered my mouth. When I turned back, Shpresa said, "Teeth!" and I had to laugh.

That really is the last thing one should forget. My head wasn't thinking. And now the teeth will stay forever useless in the glass on my nightstand.

"Maybe you should say, 'Officer, I forgot my teeth. May I please go back and get them!'" Halil said.

"Yeah, sure!" Ferid said. "He might even give you a ride back."

We all laughed at that.

A man with a *keche*, a traditional Albanian hat, looked at us nervously. He had no clue what struck us so funny. I was glad Shpresa didn't try to explain why were we laughing.

The whistle blew. The platform shook and with each vibration my fear rose. This was it. The train had come and deep down I knew it was the one-way train.

The soldiers shouted "Get in, get in!" and we all went in. The train was full and the air inside was stiff and charged with tension. There were fourteen of us in a six-seat, second-class compartment. Halil opened the window and I hungrily swallowed the cold morning air. The train started to move. I looked out the window and tried to memorize everything—the gray apartment buildings, the park with a yellow metal slide, the trees, the wooden poles, the wind hitting my face, and pigeons flying in the distance. This would be my last sight of Prishtina.

Two hours later we came to the Macedonian border and then waited five hours before we could cross. We spent twenty horrible days in a crowded tent at the Blache camp. Halil had to fight for bread and water with other refugees. Each night, before falling asleep, Shpresa would say, "That's nothing, Nana forgot her teeth," and with that she would top off any calamity she lived through that day.

I didn't mind the teeth. Without them I fit in better with other Kosovar refugees, and there was no meat to chew on anyway.

Halil's cousin arranged for us to come to America. If somebody had told me that one day I would live in America, I would have said you must be joking. Here, in Manassas, Virginia, tomatoes are not sweet, the cheese is not salty, and the bread tastes like cardboard. Still, I am content here. I am happy my family is alive and that Shpresa will go to school again. The social worker said I can get new teeth here. It will take two months, as long as it took to have them done in Yugoslavia. It is good because when they tried to send me to English classes, I said, "Not without the teeth!"

TAMARA MUSAFIA

Learning to Fight: On the Death of Lola Lucia Alvarez

M. Evelina Galang

Evelina and Lola Lucia

When I heard of the death of Lola Lucia Alvarez, I searched my notebooks, my bins of paperwork. I spun a monsoon in my little office here in Ames, Iowa. I was in search of her self-portrait, a marker drawing scratched onto a purple note card. Stuck in the middle of America, I felt so far away from her and all the lolas of LILA Pilipina (Liga na Mga Lolang Pilipina/League of Philippine Grandmothers). Perhaps I wanted to bring her to me. I found her in the pages of the summer's travel journal. She has rendered herself a messy stick figure with a cocked left foot. She has made herself a little skirt. Maybe she is dancing. For when Lola Lucia warmed up to us, young women from America, she danced. She sneaked past the gates of the Lola House and smoked a stolen cigarette with one or two of our girls. She shuffled up the hill with two of our youngest dalagas. They were clad in hip-hop jeans and too tight shirts. She wore a duster, not unlike the dress she had fashioned in her self-portrait. The three of them seemed to be running off in search of freedom, or their next pack of cigarettes. Next to her stick figure she has penned her name in blue ink—*LUCIA ALVAREZ*. On the bottom of the card there are two purple ink marks. Each of the marks has four legs. Next to one, she has written *posa*. Next to the other, she has scrawled *aso*. The pictures of the dog and cat are identical.

Lola Lucia Alvarez, unlike the other lolas we had met, lived in the Lola House on Matimtiman Street because she had no other place. Lola Regina also lives there, but that's because her home is far away in the provinces. Other lolas come to the Lola House seeking refuge from their families or their housemates. The Lola House is their community meeting place. They come when they are lonely or when the memories of war are too much to bear that day. Some come to the Lola House when they are hungry or sick. Sometimes they come looking for the LILA Pilipina staff to help them decipher legal or medical paperwork. They come one by one or several at a time. Mostly the lolas come to organize their fight, to don their armor. The lolas of LILA Pilipina-Gabriela are part of a special sisterhood. While many of them may be grandmothers, as the Pilipino word lola suggests, they are more than that. They share the wartime atrocity of being Japanese Comfort Women during World War II. Many of them were abducted when they were children as young as twelve and thirteen years of age. All of them were forced to live some time in garrisons, were raped and made into Japanese military sex slaves. The lolas gather strength from one another, have learned to fight for themselves and each other.

The lolas formally confronted their attackers and the Japanese government denied them. Undaunted, they went back to Japan and filed an appeal. This is how to seek justice with dignity. Never take no for an answer. They want an apology. They want to be compensated for the abuse they have suffered under the Japanese soldiers. Every day they relive their nightmares; every day there is a reminder. Only now are they speaking up. Only now there is strength in numbers. Some have kept their past a secret from their families most of their lives. Some have lost everything because they have come forward. Their husbands have left them. Their children are embarrassed. These loved ones don't seem to understand that this is a past they would not have chosen, a past they had no control over. Not all families, not all barrios, feel this way, but some do. There are some lolas like Lola Lucia who have died and will never be cognizant of a formal apology from Japan. Some of those lolas continue the fight through their daughters.

During the summer of 1999, while researching for *Dalaga*, a feature film about the coming of age of an American-born Filipina teenager, my students and I—Filipina Americans from the Midwest—worked with the lolas for two months. We got to know them and their everyday lives. We learned their cry for justice—LABAN! They taught us how to shout.

They took us to a rally to protest President Joseph Estrada's state-of-the-nation address. We had never been to a political rally in the Philippines. We are American-born Filipinas—all but one of us anyway. So this was exciting. Dangerous. We were told to bring what we could carry. To wear close-toed shoes. Bring water, they told us. Be ready to run.

We got to the Lola House and there were about thirty lolas gathered. They wore the purple T-shirts of LILA Pilipina-Gabriela. Scarves and straw hats protected their fragile scalps from the hot sun. The staff members passed around little bundles of food—our baon should we get hungry. Two pickled eggs, saging, rice, a bottle of water.

Driving down Commonwealth Avenue, our hearts racing, eyes searching the streets for any sign of danger, we followed two jeepneys of lolas. We watched as they hung the LILA Pilipina banner outside the truck's open doorway. The flag unfurled in the sun, wiped the sky clean of Manila smog. We could see the lolas' fists raised. They were excited too.

Someone stopped the jeepneys ahead of us. The police would not allow the drivers to continue. Only private cars were allowed to go farther. Since we had hired a van on our own, we took part in the protest by shuttling the lolas back and forth from the entrance where we expected to see President Estrada drive past.

What a sight to see the Philippine National Police (PNP) lined up, fierce as warriors set out to defend the castle. And who were they at war with? Up on the curb the police stood, their bullet-proof shields cast out in front of them, their sunglasses blocking the bright sun, their helmets keeping their heads safe from bottles or bricks or the fists of angry lolas. Below them, the lolas lined up. They set their stools down. They pulled out their signs and umbrellas. Some of them cracked salted eggs open or peeled bananas.

The lolas waited for the President. The protest program began, and all the organizations of people—workers and farmers and people of poverty—took turns at the bullhorn. They shouted their grievances to the crowd; they called out to the invisible president. Young radical poets and musicians sang songs of protest and revolution into the coveted bullhorn, accompanied by the strings of acoustic guitars. They waited for Estrada to hear their pleas. Meantime, the lolas continued to pry open their umbrellas. They baked in the sun, waiting.

I stood next to Lola Lucia that day. I held the umbrella open for her with one hand and kept my arm around her with the other. She was tired perhaps, but she was there to claim her space and make her grievances known. She had no intentions of hurting anyone. She had no intentions of leaving. When the time came, Lola Narcissa Claveria took the bullhorn in her brown hands and spoke. She commanded the attention of the crowd and that day Lola Narcissa was the voice of LILA Pilipina.

The Filipina American dalagas took turns bearing the LILA Pilipina flag. The lolas grew tired, exhausted. Lolas began to sit right down on the curb at the foot of the police. Young officers leaned over and told the lolas little jokes, flirted with them like naughty sons. One policeman called, "Take my picture, Evelyn!" Like every other Filipino I had met that summer, he had changed my name from Evelina to Evelyn. How did he know who I was? Most likely one of the lolas told him. I have a video of him waving at me, smiling. At lunchtime, the policemen's food arrived in Styrofoam take-out plates. Rice and chicken. They discarded their shields, helmets, and sunglasses like children breaking character from a game of make-believe. Their toys littered the ground. They sat down anyplace they could, their legs spread wide apart, their boyish faces smiling, as they ate their lunches.

We left the Philippines that August, our hands raised in the air, our fingers cocked into the letter *L*, and our voices singing, "Gusto kong lumaban!" I want to fight!

On Sunday, November 28, 1999, sixty lolas boarded jeepneys to protest the actions of the Third Association of Southeast Asian Nations Summit. When I hear of events that occurred at that rally, when I imagine the lolas gathering to protest the inhumane treatment they had received during WWII, when I think of how badly they wanted Japanese Prime Minister Keizo Obuchi to recognize them, I think of the way I saw the PNP that day. I think of the lolas and the way they persevered despite the heat and the exhaustion, just to make their fight known. I cannot imagine why the police would threaten to harm the lolas, though I am told they did just that.

I am told that once the lolas arrived at the Philippine International Cultural Center, they were met by a blockade of police who would not allow them to protest. Volunteers of LILA Pilipina were able to negotiate five minutes for the lolas, but as they disembarked from the jeepneys and pulled out their placards and bullhorn, PNP Officer Cabigon ordered them to evacuate. The police lined up, holding out their shields. They demanded the lolas retreat by the count of five or they would be forced to "hurt" the lolas. "Masaktan kayo!" they yelled. Some of the police were armed with guns. The lolas began moving, but they weren't moving fast enough for the police. "Tulak! Tulak!" the police yelled to one another. Ritchie Extremadura, head of LILA, told the police to be patient with the lolas. They're old, she told them, they cannot move quickly. Still they pushed and pushed. During this time, Lola Lucia was heard saying, "Ninerbyos ako dahil sa pulis." The police are making me nervous.

After the lolas boarded the jeepneys, the drivers were ordered to stay on Roxas Boulevard. The jeepneys began to take the sixty lolas away but were caught in heavy traffic. During this time more police stopped the caravan, claiming the drivers were not licensed to be in the area. They confiscated the licenses of the drivers and threatened to arrest them. The lolas told the police they could not take the drivers alone, they would have to arrest the lolas too.

The jeepneys were led to a local police station in Pasay City where the lolas took advantage of a vacant lot nearby and began their program of protest. During this time, Lola Lucia felt severe pains in her neck and head. When staff members requested that the police release one of the drivers to take Lola Lucia to the hospital, they refused, saying it was not their commander's orders. She would have to wait.

The PNP detained Lola Lucia fifteen minutes more after her attack.

Finally, a staff member of LILA was able to secure a taxi and took Lola Lucia to San Juan de Dios Hospital in Pasay City. Even as she was being taken to ICU, Lola Lucia was saying, "Gusto kong lumaban!" I want to fight! Shortly after her arrival at the hospital, Lola Lucia slipped into her five-day coma.

Many of the lolas are angry at the treatment and abuse of this incident. Lola Anastacia Fortes said, "We witnessed the same violence, the same brutality we suffered in the hands of the Japanese soldiers. We were once more stripped of our dignity." Lola Fedencia David added, "We want justice. What does the Estrada government give us in return? Estrada has not in any way extended his support to the lolas, now he has responded to our cries with violence, with further injustice. He gives first-class treatment to his foreign guests and treats us like rags, he treats us like criminals. Perhaps he is unaware that he is host to a Prime Minister of a nation, who is more of a criminal, as Japan still refuses to recognize the crimes committed against humanity over fifty-four years ago."

The five dalagas are now scattered across America—San Francisco, Chicago, Virginia Beach, and here I am in Ames, Iowa. We have been conversing electronically. We remember Lola Lucia's voice, soft and textured with age and years of smoking. We remember her unassuming manner, how she gradually joined us in our activities, painting her image on canvas, writing her letters to Japan. She always began in Tagalog, and in her excitement she'd slip into Visayan, her native dialect. And somehow it was always the dalaga who didn't speak Pilipino at all who attempted to translate her letters.

With no money, no house of her own, Lola Lucia paid for her room and board at the Lola House by running errands for LILA Pilipina. During our stay in the Philippines, she got close to the dalagas for they'd join her on her walks. Or they'd sneak off with her to have a cigarette. Or they'd dance with her in the company of the other lolas.

I once pulled her across the Lola House patio, begging her to participate in a drama. She finally agreed and played the part of Tara's novio. The lolas teased her, "What kind of boyfriend waves a paypay?" Laughing, she tossed it aside, and then she spent the rest of the drama giggling and wiping the perspiration from her forehead with her hanky. She needed her paypay.

I told Lola Lucia I'd leave her my pink umbrella because she had burned a cigarette hole in hers and the leak was streaming monsoon rains right next to her tiny face. What sort of umbrella was that? It was rainy season. She should have a new one. Or at least a bright pink one. I forgot to leave it. Even as I was boarding the plane that August, I felt I had let her down somehow. She was still running around with that ridiculous umbrella. Old, dirty, leaking umbrella.

There was no money for her burial, or for the time she stayed at the hospital.

In protest of the actions of the PNP, LILA Pilipina-Gabriela has filed a complaint with the Commission of Human Rights. They are demanding an investigation of the PNP's behavior. They are demanding the police take responsibility for Lola Lucia's death. They are looking for the resignation of the head of the police and they are asking for funding to cover the cost of Lola Lucia's burial and the medication she needed while in the hospital.

Lola's self-portrait

It is hard to hear this news from halfway across the world. It's hard to be in the middle of America when my heart is sitting on the open-air patio of the Lola House in Quezon City. I have been flipping through my photos from that summer, holding tight to every photo I have of Lola Lucia. Her self-portrait sits next to me even now. I am itching to do something for her. I am dying to carry on the fight. I am writing to you, hoping somehow this will make a difference for Lola Lucia Alvarez and all the lolas who are seeking justice not only from the Japanese government, but from their own. I am holding my hands up in front of me, making *L*'s out of my thumbs and index fingers. I am calling out "LABAN!" Can you hear me?

M. EVELINA GALANG

Author's footnote: The supervising Police Officer of the Philippine National Police, Manuel Cabigon, was brought up on charges on the death of Lola Lucia Alvarez, but because of government bureaucracy and the change of administration, his cases in the Pasay City Court District and Congress are pending. Rechilda Extremadura, LILA Pilipina coordinator, feels our letter writing campaign, international pressure, motivated the government to press charges. The lolas' appeal to the Japanese Circuit Courts regarding the wartime atrocities against the surviving WWII Filipina Comfort Women was denied on December 6, 2000. They filed the case with the Japanese Supreme Court on December 20, 2000, and are waiting to see if the courts will hear their case.

CABEZA

MONIQUE DE VARENNES

None of them, not even Barbara herself, quite understood why she brought the pig's head home from the market. She had browsed in the meat department's hooves-and-hearts section many times—Variety Meats, it was euphemistically called—but she had never before been tempted to buy. For one thing, she had no idea how to cook the innards and extremities whose red or pink or tannish flesh jammed the display case. For another, she had always felt that looking was quite enough.

And she did look, nearly every time she visited the market. She loved the colors and textures of the meat: the deep red coils of spleen, the lacy tripe, the kidneys like weighty, dark bunches of grapes. She liked to see the thick slabs of tongue, so surprisingly large and muscular that she wondered how they fit in an animal's mouth, and the pigs' feet, small and achingly dainty, like a society matron's helpless, manicured hand.

The pig's head, though, was altogether different. It was the first one Barbara had ever seen in Variety Meats, and it had her attention from the moment she laid eyes on it. It had belonged to a young pig, a piglet, she surmised, for it was not very big. Whitish, sightless, it wore an expression of great seriousness, as if it fully recognized the gravity of its situation. It seemed isolated there in the case, separated by shrink-wrap from the neat neighboring packages of organs and hocks, some of which were undoubtedly its own. It looked lonely even, and impulsively Barbara popped it into her shopping cart.

Driving home, she smiled with pleasure at the thought of her purchase. No exile in the dark recesses of the meat keeper for this baby; she would make a place for it at the very center of things.

But even when she had settled the head front and center on the refrigerator's middle shelf, pushing jars and leftovers aside with rare abandon, she felt that something was missing. The pig looked as mournful of countenance and as forlorn as ever.

Barbara got busy. She brought out a white serving plate, and, stripping off the head's wrappings, set it carefully in the center. Some lettuce leaves gave color to the dish, and she accented the green with a sprinkling of cherry tomatoes. Briefly she considered stuffing an apple into the pig's mouth, but she discarded the idea: it would give the head far too rakish an air. Still, she could not resist draping one sprig of parsley over the pig's right ear.

She set the plate in the refrigerator and stepped back a few paces to contemplate the effect. The pig looked less gloomy now—almost cheerful, in fact. And if its gaiety seemed somewhat forced, well, at least she knew she had tried her best. Satisfied with the disposition of the head, she closed the refrigerator door and forgot about it entirely.

Two hours later, hearing the kitchen door slap shut behind her fourteen-year-old, Barbara remembered. No greeting, of course. No call of inquiry, drifting down to the basement where Barbara folded laundry; Carol had abandoned such pleasantries a good two years earlier. She now communicated rarely, except to express displeasure. Upstairs, kitchen cabinets slammed as she hunted for an after-school snack.

Barbara dropped the T-shirt she was smoothing out and rushed to the foot of the basement stairs. "Carol, honey, before you open the refrigerator, there's something I—"

But she was too late. Carol's shriek ripped through the air, a blade of sound. Barbara dashed upstairs. She found Carol standing squarely in front of the refrigerator, her eyes fixed on the closed metal door. Barbara put awkward arms around her daughter.

"What is that? Mom, what's in there?" Carol demanded, shaking free of her mother.

"It's a pig's head—a piglet's, really. I bought it at Ralphs."

The words sounded strange to Barbara. Clearly they sounded strange to Carol as well, for she gave her mother one brief, dark look and fled abruptly from the room. A moment later, Barbara heard a door slam in the far reaches of the house. She opened the refrigerator.

There sat the head, all innocence, clearly incapable of hurting even a fly. Really, she couldn't see why Carol was raising such a fuss. In any case, she had no time to contemplate the question now. There were piles of laundry still to fold, then there was dinner to be made. She thought pork chops would be nice, though she realized the choice showed a certain lack of sensitivity. She would serve them on a lovely bed of saffron rice.

It was not Barbara's habit to make the same mistake twice, and as five-thirty neared she kept alert for the sound of the garage door. Jed she did not have to worry about, at least not yet; he had soccer practice nearly every afternoon during the season and rarely made it home much before dinner. But she did not want Peter to be surprised. Her husband did not do well with surprises. She settled down distractedly for a look at the newspaper.

It was nearly six when she heard the sound of Peter's car. Barbara folded the paper neatly, taking care to smooth out the creases she had made, then wandered as casually as she could into the kitchen. Carol must have been listening for Peter too, for when Barbara entered, her daughter was already there, and Peter, briefcase in hand, was bending close to hear her whispered voice.

"A what?" he exclaimed. He did not seem to notice that Barbara had come into the room.

"A pig's head, Daddy—I swear. She got it at Ralphs. Check it out for yourself."

Peter opened the refrigerator impatiently, as if anticipating some particularly stupid prank. Then a small sound escaped him, something between a grunt and a groan, and his back slowly stiffened. He stood absolutely still. After eighteen years of marriage Barbara knew that silence, that utter stillness; he was busy rearranging the unpleasant into some form that suited him better.

After a moment he seemed to shake himself, and he reached in for the pitcher of whiskey sours that Barbara always had waiting for him when he came home from work. "Well, Carol," he said finally, "I don't see that this is anything to get excited about." His voice was bland. "Your mother is probably planning to make cabeza."

Carol's pointed, freckled face sharpened a bit in disappointment. Clearly she had hoped for a scene. "Cabeza?" she repeated sullenly. "What's that?"

"A traditional Spanish dish—a kind of stew, I believe."

"She's planning to cook it? To make us eat it?"

"I never said I was going to cook it. Never uttered a word about that," put in Barbara, who had begun chopping up a crisp napa cabbage. The pork was baking nicely. But they did not seem to hear her.

"Well, she can cook it any way she wants," Carol continued. "I'm not touching it."

"Touching what?" Jed banged in the kitchen door and swung his backpack to the floor.

"Look in the refrigerator for a preview of tomorrow's dinner. Mom's going Spanish on us."

Jed followed Carol's suggestion, gazing for a moment into the antiseptic brightness of the refrigerator. Then he reached behind the head for a bottle of Gatorade. "Weird," he murmured appreciatively. "When Mom's done, can I have the skull for my room?"

Not much more was said about the pig's head that evening; Peter effectively glowered them all into silence. But it was he who brought up the subject as Barbara was getting ready for bed. She knew what he planned to discuss from the moment he cleared his throat. Stretched out on the mattress, his reading glasses perched atop his head like a second set of ears, he had the same look of strained forbearance he'd worn the day he had dissuaded her from filing for divorce, three years earlier. His voice, when he spoke, was low and calm. "About the cow's head, honey—"

"Pig's head," Barbara corrected promptly. "It's a pig."

"About the pig's head. Are you planning to cook it or not? Because if you're planning to cook it, I personally will eat it and encourage the kids to do the same. But if you're not, I think you ought to consider—" and here he appeared to be sorting rather carefully through his words "—disposing of the thing."

Barbara received this suggestion in noncommittal silence, though her bones froze at the thought of throwing away her pig. She watched Peter's face grow increasingly intense, and she knew he was struggling with something. "Why did you buy it?" he blurted out at last.

Barbara considered this for the first time, rather surprised that it had not occurred to her to wonder until now. She did not dare tell him that the pig had looked lonely, and that was not, she guessed, the whole truth in any case. "I don't know," she said finally.

For a moment she thought, I should try to talk to him about it. Who else, after all? The children were still too young, and no one outside the family could possibly understand. She looked at him, exposed on the bed, his rough, hairy legs poking out from smooth pajama bottoms, his stomach wearing the soft bulge of middle age. He looked vulnerable, approachable. Then his face hardened, and that was all she could see.

"Never mind why you bought it," he said gruffly. "I don't even know why I asked. Just deal with it, Barbara, won't you?" He flicked his glasses down from his forehead to cover his eyes again, as if closing himself to any further conversation. And that was that.

Next morning, Barbara noticed that the upstairs bathrooms needed cleaning, and she spent a couple of hours working on them. She was the sort of housekeeper who always let things get a little disreputable before she cleaned, so she could experience the small satisfaction of seeing her scrubbing and polishing make a difference.

Later, over a sandwich, Barbara paged through her cookbooks, looking for a recipe for cabeza. She was not quite sure that such a thing existed. She knew that the word meant head in Spanish. She also knew that Peter was quite capable of inventing a dish if it helped smooth over an awkward moment in his day. Certainly none of her foreign cookbooks—of which she had several, left over from the days when she had truly enjoyed her time in the kitchen—made reference to it. The *Larousse Gastronomique* came closest, with one recipe for brains, one for the snout, and no fewer than eight ways of fixing the ears.

The very thought of cutting into the pig's head aroused anxiety, and Barbara brought the platter out onto the kitchen table and sat down in front of it. Today it looked scoured and sere and somehow wise. Peter was right to ask: Why had she bought it?

She stared at it hard, trying to understand. Its presence seemed to overflow the kitchen. It was, for her, utterly there, more than her cookbooks or the salt shaker or the Pothos on the windowsill, whose small green life she had nursed for nearly fifteen years. She was aware that the head aroused in her a tangle of feelings, and that those feelings were quite strong. But when she tried to separate them so that she could name them—name even one—they eluded her, vanishing in wisps of emotional fog.

She looked at her watch—an entire hour gone. There would barely be time to throw some caramel custard together before Carol got home from school. Barbara thought she would make a double batch; caramel custard was Carol's favorite.

By the time she heard her daughter's step on the driveway, Barbara was a bit apprehensive. But to her surprise Carol did not seem inclined to be hostile. "Did you cook the head yet?" she asked bluntly.

Barbara shook her head.

"Well, that's a relief." Carol sniffed the air avidly; she still had a child's unerring radar for sugar. "Hey, something smells sweet."

"Caramel custard. It's for dessert tonight, but there's extra, if you'd like a snack. In the refrigerator."

Barbara watched Carol's mouth tighten as she contemplated the refrigerator uneasily. She smiled a bit as her daughter pulled open the door and quickly withdrew a dish of custard. This Carol bore off, wordlessly, to her room.

That night neither Peter nor Jed mentioned the pig's head, though both of them asked, almost upon entering and with enormous wariness, what was for dinner.

"Chicken," Barbara answered primly, and each refrained from commenting on what she had not cooked.

The next morning, as soon as the last of her family had left the house, Barbara took out the head again. A faint odor had begun to emanate from it and its garnish was past its prime. Barbara removed the wilted greens (the tomatoes were still serviceable) and sprinkled a little Arm & Hammer on the plate before tenderly laying a new bed of fresh lettuce. She patted the top of its skull. "You might smell a little off, but you look just fine," she reassured the piglet, smiling at it warmly. Then she wrapped it in heavy layers of Saran Wrap and returned it to its shelf in the fridge.

She did not take it out again, but the knowledge that it was there eased her through the day. She greeted Carol that afternoon with a plate of freshly baked cookies.

"You're cooking a lot these days," her daughter commented as she filled a glass with tap water.

"For some reason I've just been in a kitchen mood." Barbara registered the water in her daughter's hand. "Don't you want some milk?" she asked solicitously. "I was thinking as I baked these cookies how tasty they'd be with a tall, foamy glass of milk."

"No, this'll be okay." Carol's eyes jerked nervously toward the refrigerator, and Barbara could see that she had no intention of opening that door. So, helpfully, she threw it open herself, revealing the gleaming shelves, the milk carton, the pig's head. "Come on, have a glass."

When Carol had retired—rather abruptly, Barbara thought—to her room, it occurred to her that no one had been visiting the refrigerator much, not since the head had come home. Last night, Jed hadn't made his usual late-night food raid. And Peter hadn't even gone for his nightly whiskey sour; she had found the pitcher untouched on its shelf this morning.

Her observation about the refrigerator was confirmed that evening at dinner, when it became clear that she had not set out horseradish for the pot roast. This combination was traditional in their family; Peter had been known to become quite irritable if they were out of the condiment on pot roast night. But tonight no one mentioned the missing horseradish. It was always, of course, possible that they did not notice, but somehow Barbara doubted it. She sat in quiet amazement, watching her uncomplaining family eat their pot roast unadorned.

The evening passed without incident. Only Peter mentioned the head, commenting in an offhand way that she might want to make that cabeza soon if she was planning to cook it at all; he didn't think that kind of meat had much of a shelf life. Barbara responded with an alert and agreeable nod.

She had noted with interest that the family was tiptoeing around her, humoring her. Peter was his usual reserved self, yet there was a guarded solicitude in his treatment of her that she had never noticed before. Jed, the charmer of the group, had begun to favor her with doses of his incredible smile. Even Carol had been almost polite. Barbara wandered through this atmosphere in a mild fog, curious as to what would happen next.

Three days passed. No one spoke to her about the head. One morning she got up early and, as always these days, went straight to the kitchen. Even before she opened the refrigerator, she could smell it. The odor was stronger now, and it was not pleasant. She pulled out the platter and, holding her breath just a bit, patted a thick layer of Arm & Hammer on every surface of the head. It gave the thing a ghostly look but seemed to tamp down the odor considerably.

Barbara had long ago abandoned the garnishes that surrounded it. The lettuce lay flat and black on the plate, the tomatoes were dimpled with softening dark spots, and the once jaunty parsley was little more than a smear along the piglet's cheek. Ignoring this, she doubled the sheath of Saran Wrap, masking the smell.

By the time Jed came in she had coffee going. A bowl of pancake batter was at the ready by the side of the stove. She could tell from a tightening around his eyes that he smelled the pig too, but still he offered her his rich smile. "So, Mom, you want to come to my soccer game this morning? Dad and Carol are coming, and we're thinking of going out to lunch after."

"Oh, I couldn't possibly. I'm making a terrine of veal for dinner and it takes forever. If I don't start early we won't eat till midnight. Besides, isn't this a school day?"

"No, Mom," Jed said gently, "it's Saturday. Come on—you haven't been to a game for ages. It'll do you good to sit out in the sun. We can have burgers for dinner, for all I care."

But Barbara demurred. She had too much to do here, she insisted; the dinner ingredients were bought already. Besides, she had seen him play a hundred games and would see a hundred more—she could miss just one. Finally, Jed was forced to relent.

Barbara enjoyed her day. When the kitchen had been cleared of breakfast things, she set a pot of spices simmering on the stove to freshen the air. With the cheerful bubbling in the background she made her stuffing, chopped and marinated her meat, lined her terrine with pork fat, and artfully filled it with layers of the stuffing and veal and ham. It was the first time in ages that she had taken real pleasure in cooking. She glazed oranges for dessert while the terrine baked, and while it cooled, made arranged salads and cold rice. It would be the perfect light supper for her family.

They all, however, displayed a striking lack of appetite for dinner. They talked loudly—with more animation than usual, Barbara thought—but they only picked sporadically at their food. Perhaps they had eaten too much, or too late, at lunchtime. It was fortunate that she'd decided on a cold dinner, one that would keep—for days, if necessary—in the refrigerator.

That night, Barbara went to bed early. But the sound of crying pierced her dreams, and with a mother's instinct she got up, stumbling across the darkened bedroom, to offer comfort. The light was on in Carol's room. Even from Barbara's doorway down the hall she could hear her daughter's voice, raised in weepy complaint. Was she babbling to someone on the phone at this hour? A small twist of annoyance infiltrated Barbara's concern.

As she approached the door, Carol's words came clearer. "It's just so weird. She spends all of this time cooking—cakes, cookies, fancy dinners. And there's that head, just rotting in the refrigerator. It scares me, Daddy." She sobbed loudly, her breath ratcheting.

Barbara felt excitement trickle through her, and was invigorated. Crouching in the dark hall just outside the doorway, she settled in to listen.

"I know it seems odd," Peter replied, his voice steeled to calmness, "but you have to look at this from your mother's perspective. She bought the head to cook it, naturally, and for some reason she just hasn't. Maybe she's embarrassed about that. And—"

"And what, Dad?" Jed broke in. So it was a full family conference. "And she just leaves it to rot? Face it, Dad, there's something wrong with this picture. Mom's gone over the edge."

There was silence for a moment; then Jed spoke again, his voice strained and determined. "I don't know about the two of you, but I'm not eating another thing that's been sitting in there with that head. And first thing tomorrow I'm going to talk to Mom. I'm going to find out what she's been thinking. This is crazy, going on like this, pretending nothing is wrong."

Carol began to cry again. This time, Barbara could hear real pain in her sobs. She knew that Carol's face would be red and slick with unwiped tears, that her shoulders would be heaving, that her hands, forgotten, would lie limp at her sides. It was the way she had always cried as a child. As far as Barbara knew, she had not cried that way for years. How nice that she could still feel things so deeply.

But Peter ignored Carol. "I think you're blowing things out of proportion," he told Jed. "And I don't want you bringing this up with your mom." An edge had come into his voice, and he paused for a moment. Barbara could see his back from where she crouched; it twitched almost imperceptibly. When Peter spoke again his tone was neutral. "Sometimes it's better just to let things pass, to let them resolve themselves on their own. If you talked to her you might—"

"Might what, Dad?" Jed demanded. "I don't understand. Might what?"

"Leave it alone, Jed," Peter said harshly. "You're too young to understand the damage you might do." He turned away abruptly and stared out into the hall. Barbara was sure he had sensed her presence—he was looking straight at her. She cringed a little farther into the darkness. Then she saw that his eyes were focused inward. As she watched, his facial muscles began to work crazily, convulsively, and for a moment it looked as if he were about to cry. Then his features congealed into a rictus of pain and woe.

Barbara knew that for this moment, at least, he saw it all—that with their life stripped for this brief time of all its custom he was forced to see it: the dry boneyard of their existence. Pleasure coursed through her like a river breaking onto a parched plain. It swelled her, and she luxuriated. And in this moment of fulfillment she knew: this was what she had wanted. This was what the pig was for.

Yet even as she exulted, Peter's expression was changing again. Fascinated, she watched him as slowly and with great effort he forced his features back into their normal aspect of impenetrable calm. He turned back to the children. "Listen to me, both of you. Carol, stop your crying now. We will have to be very kind to your mother." He spoke slowly, deliberately. "Very kind for a long, long time."

Sensing that the conference was close to an end, Barbara slipped down the dark hallway, back to her bed. She closed her eyes, feigning sleep, and it engulfed her, closing over her like the dark waters of the sea.

The next morning, the pig's head was gone. One by one the family ventured tentatively into the kitchen, to be greeted by the sight of Barbara on her knees, scrubbing out the refrigerator. Air freshener spread its artificial comfort; homemade Belgian waffles warmed in the oven.

Peter, concerned that the head might draw ants, slipped out to the trash bins behind the garage to see that it was properly wrapped. But there was no sign of the pig. It did not occur to him to search the yard. There, deep behind the rhododendrons that marked the farthest reaches of their property, he might have seen a mound of freshly turned earth, the *Larousse* laid upon it like a tombstone.

For a while, things improved. Barbara felt herself at the very center of her family, as she had been when the children were infants. There was a strained quality to Peter's concern, and to the children's attempts to include her in their lives, but Barbara did not mind, knowing as she did how conscious effort could grow in time into habit.

But then, in the way that families have, they abandoned their efforts, drifting slowly back to the patterns they were accustomed to. Barbara could feel their relief as they reverted. She tried to insert herself into their conversations and their plans, but she had become invisible again, inaudible. And the triumph she had felt the night of the family conference was lost to her.

One afternoon Carol came home and found her mother absent. Everything else was as it should be, but it was disturbing that there was no note, no explanation. Barbara had not returned by the time Peter came home from work, nor when Jed banged his way in the back door. No smell of dinner rose to meet them, and they wandered the house edgily, murmuring to one another.

At last, around 7:30, Barbara's car pulled into the driveway. "I can't believe how late it is," she sang as she entered the kitchen. Her voice, unnaturally cheery, drew them into the room.

"Let me help you with those," Jed offered, indicating the collection of Ralphs' bags around her knees. They were jammed with food.

"Oh, that's all right. They're not that heavy." With a protective gesture, and grinning a little crazily, Barbara stepped in front of the bags. "Just look at the time! If everyone will clear out and give me some room, I'll get dinner going. It's something we haven't had for a while. Something Spanish."

Efficiently, Barbara lifted the bags to the counter. No one else moved. They watched as if hypnotized as Barbara unloaded groceries: bright tomatoes; smooth, golden onions; a green profusion of limes, cilantro, and jalapeno. Then, what they were waiting for—a large package wrapped in butcher paper.

She unwrapped it slowly, eyeing them provocatively, and lifting the bundle of whitish flesh to her nose, she inhaled deeply. "Lovely!" she exclaimed. "The freshest snapper Ralphs has had in ages. You all liked snapper soup the last time I made it, didn't you?"

And she began to laugh. Oh, it was a terrible sound—she knew it was terrible. Her family's faces, horror-struck, confirmed it. Still, she could not stop. Wave after wave of hysterics assailed her until at last her knees buckled and she dropped unceremoniously to the floor. This set her off even more. Her throat ached from howling and her ribs felt as if they might crack.

The children were backing away from her, aghast, but Peter edged in closer, the expression on his face, all twisted again as it had been that other time, too comical to bear. She choked a bit, recovered, and then, unexpectedly, hiccupped. The laughter that this inspired nearly did her in. She rocked back and forth on the linoleum, red-faced and tear-stained and heaving helplessly. And as she rocked she wondered, with that small part of her brain still rooted to consciousness, if she would ever be able to stop.

MONIQUE DE VARENNES

The last measures of Handel's *Water Music* came to rest, and Robin locked the door of the shell shop from the inside, took her father's flashlight, and descended through the trap door to the tunnel leading to the sea cave. Several steps down she heard banging on the door. Through the store window she saw Lana, still in a T-shirt even though her concert was in two hours.

Robin came back up and opened the shop door. "Don't you have to get ready or go over your music?"

"Nah." Lana let the screen door slam behind her.

"*Nah*? How can you love music and not *want* to think about it every spare minute?"

"Listen, I have this terrific idea," Lana said. "A big bash for the end of high school. Right here." She grinned the grin of big plans.

"In the shop?"

"Du-uh. In the cave. That way, no parents."

Robin's throat caught fire. How could Lana say that and not realize? "Your hair's a mess. Want me to French braid it?"

"Sure." Lana plunked herself down behind the shell jewelry counter.

"How about six braids this time, all coiling into a loose knot on top?"

Lana handed Robin her brush. "Don't you get it? You're always whining about not getting invited places. Now you'll be the center of attention. It'll be your party. All you have to do is let us in and be your sweet, gorgeous, weird little self."

"My weird little self tells me not to trust you."

Two couples and a little boy came in and asked what there was to see in the cave. Robin pointed to pictures of it on the wall.

"What's the history of this place?" one of the men asked.

She pulled the brush in several long, rough strokes until Lana yelped. If she started far enough back, maybe they'd get bored and go down before they heard it all.

While she braided, she told them a train from San Diego brought tourists to La Jolla at the turn of the century, and the railroad owners charged money to lower people down on ropes over the cliffs above the cave's entrance. "Later they hired boys to dive off a board 150 feet above the water. People paid to see that too until one of them was killed."

They were listening but they weren't reaching for their wallets. She knew it took horror to make people pay the dollar-and-a-half cave entrance fee, so she had to go on. Just say the words, she told herself. Be like a player piano.

"Once, for a hundred dollars, one diver doused himself with oil, set himself on fire, and jumped. People saw a human ball of flame plunge into the sea and then come up and walk away."

"What's that bone?" the boy asked, pointing.

Robin kept her eyes on Lana's hair. "A horse's jawbone." It had been mounted over the trap door so people would ask. She wanted to take it down but couldn't. She and Grandmother Hattie needed the money it made.

"I think he means, what's it doing there," his father said.

Robin let the braids fall through her fingers. If the boy were any younger, she'd say she didn't know. She felt the grip of their waiting faces. She tried to take her mind some place else and just give the spiel, but there was Lana.

"On New Year's Day 1900, the tunnel to the cave was opened to visitors. A huge crowd came on the train. There was a very low tide. The promoters, not *my* family, but the people my grandmother's father bought the cave from, charged admission for an event." She pointed out the window uphill to her house. "Imagine that as a corral. Everyone lined up side by side behind two ropes facing each other with a space between that made an alley from the corral to the end of the point. There was one horse in the corral, with a blindfold on.

"When they took it off, they whipped that horse until he was crazy. He reared up and snorted, his nostrils flared, his tail thrashed. He kept kicking and crashing into the fence, but there was no way he could get away from those whips. They opened the gate and he bolted through the alley and the people ran after him shouting. They whipped that horse all the way out to the point until he flew off the cliff in a big arc, pawing the air, and broke apart on the rocks below."

Her throat tightened to a string. "People heard his bones crack. Like gunfire, some said. They watched his jaw open and shut, open and shut, slower and slower until sundown. The waves washed red around him, but his body would not wash out to sea. For days seagulls pecked flesh off the bones until the skeleton eventually fell apart. Months afterward bones kept coming ashore and lodging in the rocks in the cave." She felt sick to say the next part. "For a long time people went down into the cave just to look for them, to keep as collector's items. There was even an auction for the hooves. They only found three."

She couldn't look at the boy. Lana was staring at her openmouthed. Well, she might understand something now. The bones in the sea. Having to repeat it to keep people coming. Grandmother Hattie's only income.

The women shook their heads. The men murmured disgust and then paid for the cave entrance—the intended result.

After the people went down, Robin and Lana were quiet. Robin stroked the smooth hair on the top of Lana's head a few times.

"I never knew. I'd never heard the whole story."

Robin put out her hand to stop what Lana might say next. She anchored the braids in loose, interwoven coils using bobby pins with tiny polished white cowries that the shop sold. "They'll look like pearls under the stage lights."

"It looks fantastic," Lana said. "Think about the party and tell me tomorrow. Who else has a *cave* to party in?" Lana hugged her quickly. "You're one of a kind," she called over her shoulder, and let the door bang again.

Robin locked it and sat awhile, picking at a chapped place on her lip. Then she went down into the musty tunnel. A breeze funneled up the dank passageway, and she felt the relief of cool air. The roar of the surf leapt up the tunnel. Like a French horn, she thought, and a timpani, and then a cymbal crash. In Handel's *Water Music* there was all that answering back and forth—the horns answering the strings, the strings echoing the harpsichord, like a busy, happy conversation, like a party. She missed being in the school orchestra. In eighth grade Lana was already first chair violin while she had sat in paradise in the last row of the seconds. She was in Heaven again when she and Lana played the Bach double. Before every lesson she used to take a calm bath and think about every measure. And now Lana was roaming around town thinking about anything but music right before her concert.

Angrily, she dumped out the small trash containers bolted to the tunnel under each electrical light. At the wooden platform in the big cavern, she leaned over the railing to feel the spray against her face. Waves always soothed her. She could count on them. When one went out, another was sure to come in. The cavern filled and emptied, filled and emptied, breathing liquid in and out over the cranberry velvet algae, like Neptune's lung.

A pigeon flew in carrying a twig in his beak. She showed the family several nests in crevices where they were sitting on eggs, and some crabs scuttling over rocks. She fanned her father's flashlight across the beautiful smear of red iron oxide that reminded her of a sunset on a smoggy day. The bands of white Epsom salt were like lines of surf.

She turned to face the platform. Plenty big for a party. *In the cave. That way, no parents.*

How convenient.

Lana didn't even know what she said. Robin forgave her.

Now wouldn't that be a twisted fairy tale: weird Robin Hatfield who likes the wrong music, sees the wrong movies, says the wrong things, gives a terrific party, and lives happily ever after loved by dozens of friends.

Not likely.

What if no one talked to her? The little weirdo who spends her afternoons in a cave.

The cave belonged to the pigeons anyway.

Walking back up with the couples, she shined the light into a side cavern floored in miniature limestone terraces. Orange and creamy stalactites glistened. She aimed the beam on the side wall for the boy to see. "Guess what this is called." Deep brown minerals looking like hot fudge had dripped in tendrils over the shiny cream-colored limestone. "Ice Cream Sundae."

"Yeah," he said, stretching out the word in awe, which made her happy.

"Don't lick it," she teased.

When they came up through the trap door, the older woman said, "You're so young to be doing all this by yourself."

"I've been practically running the place for four years."

In eighth grade, when Grandmother Hattie couldn't manage the stairs any more, Hattie had told her that she'd have to do all the cave work and help with the shell shop or they'd have to close them. Unthinkable, so she'd gone down to clean the cave even though she was afraid she'd find a bone lodged in the rocks. And, because the cave wasn't enough of a tourist attraction without its gruesome history, she took over from Hattie the telling of the stories, even though the first time, she threw up behind the counter and didn't sleep that night. She couldn't explain it to anybody. Those lives. As if they were nothing.

She watched the mother pick up a Fluted Giant Clam, one of her favorites. Every millimeter of growth left its mark, like rings on a tree. Then the woman examined a polished Chambered Nautilus, a mother-of-pearl spiral of larger and larger homes. Robin liked to think the animal grew a new one only when he was good and ready. The boy chose a starfish and his mother settled on a common polished abalone. All its crusty character and history had been ground off.

"It'll be a nice soap dish, don't you think?" the mother said.

Robin shrugged. While she was wrapping them, she slipped in a turban shell the boy had turned over and over in his hand.

She unlocked the outside door, followed them out, and walked under the eucalyptus trees to home. Hattie was already dressed for the concert, wearing her dark blue dress, the same one she'd worn to the memorial service. She hadn't bought anything new since. After dinner they walked along Coast Boulevard to the art museum where Lana's recital was.

Where the sidewalk came close to the sea, Hattie stopped. Not to look at tide pools. Or to watch a wave. Or a pelican. She just stopped. To breathe. But they were going downhill. A sign to both of them. Robin pretended not to notice.

"I think this is where Doc in *Cannery Row* came to gather octopi," Robin said, just to say *something*. She had read that part in school a dozen times, trying to figure out exactly where along this shoreline he did his collecting. Steinbeck described how the refuse of the sea, broken shells and bits of skeleton, all made the bottom of the ocean into a fantastic cemetery.

And right then, in the novel, Doc found the body of a young girl wedged, face up, in a rock crevice. Like the horse's bones. Doc said the girl's face looked up at him through the water and her hair washed gently about her head. Robin had nightmares about the girl's eyes open underwater. She wondered if people who fell from a burning airplane into the sea might turn face up and have a last look upwards through the water at the sky. It would be unfair to tell Hattie that. She only hoped that for Mom and Dad, the moment of falling might have felt like a movie not happening to them.

Robin had asked Hattie if Lana could play Grieg's *Solveig's Song* at their memorial service, and Hattie had said, "Anything you like, honey." Lana had borrowed a white choir robe and sat at the end of the point with the sea behind her and the wind billowing out the wide sleeves like angel wings. The notes seemed to sob *for* Robin. After everyone left, Robin made her play it over and over until the notes drained away and there was only love. When the sun set, she walked out to the cliff edge, and because she had read that ancient people put shells in tombs to give comfort to the dead, she threw into the sea two shells from the store—a True Heart's Cockle for Mom and a Lazarus Jewel Box for Dad, his favorite, he'd said, because its spiny folds made safe homes for smaller creatures.

After that, people treated her differently, with a kind of pity that set her apart. Sort of mothery smothery. Even Lana. Her English teacher gave her an A on her Steinbeck report, a grade she didn't deserve. Her violin teacher demanded less from her so she skipped practices. She couldn't get the strings to sob like Lana did, or like she felt. There were only the notes. She couldn't get the feel. And then there was the shop to run. At the end of the year, in spite of what she knew would be Mom's wishes, she dropped out of the orchestra.

Tonight the audience in the museum auditorium was mixed. Rich La Jollans always showed up for every benefit, this time for Lana's study at the Royal Academy of Music in London. Lana's friends from school and from the orchestra were there too. Robin knew them, but she was not of them. They had cars and money and time to party, a clan as tight as their parents' tennis clubs. Hattie pushed her forward to talk to them, saying she wanted to go in and sit down.

Lana's boyfriend, Jim, was holding a bunch of red roses. She wondered what it would be like to have a boyfriend, someone she could be off her guard with.

"Nice flowers," she said.

"I heard about the party," Trent Reardon said.

She whirled around. "Lana told you?"

"Cool place for a party. The cave."

"I haven't agreed yet."

"But you vill, my darlink. Vere I come from, in Transylvania, ve always have the parties in caves. The darker the better."

She'd always liked Trent, especially when he did his silly villain imitations. Now he asked her the worst thing, where she was going to school next year.

"Depends on where you're going."

"No, really." He was turning dangerously serious.

"Certainly not where Lana's going."

"The truth, Robin."

"The truth Robin is that I haven't applied."

"You've got to be kidding! You've always been smart. Remember that geography project in junior high?"

She remembered all right. She had mounted shells all around a map of the world, with strings attached to pins showing the places where they were found. "Five Hundred Million Years of Design," she called it. After her oral report, the teacher asked how she knew so much about shells, and Trent had called out, "She sells seashells by the seashore," and everyone had laughed.

"I hate him," she told Lana that night on the phone.

"No, you don't. You've got a crush is all."

Whatever it was, she couldn't keep up the hate, or the crush, or much of anything else connected with school. Deadlines for college applications just slipped by.

When the lights dimmed in the lobby, Trent said, "Come sit with us."

"I can't. I'm with my grandmother." Flushing hot and with a sudden dryness in her throat, she made her way down the aisle to sit by Hattie who patted her hand when the lights went out.

Lana came on stage in a tight black dress with no back, mesh stockings, and platform shoes. Her hair *was* fantastic. The cowries made Robin feel that something of her was on that stage. Lana waved her bow as if it were a magic wand, nuzzled against the chin rest in that sexy way of hers, and began with Mozart. Robin closed her eyes and let the music enter her. Each selection got more and more camp until Lana was prancing around to a Sting song and twitching her bottom to "Your Cheating Heart." She ended with a tough Paganini piece, full of impossible pizzicato. It left Robin breathless.

Lana gave the audience a cool, triumphant smile and executed a deep, slow, elegant bow.

"She has a natural touch," Hattie said over the applause.

"She takes it for granted," Robin snapped, clapping until her palms stung.

She would gladly have sacrificed big things, impossible things, like the cave, or even love, to play that well. By comparison, what had she accomplished? Just keeping the cave open for the last four years. And where was she headed?

She didn't know.

The next day she stopped Lana in the quad. "You were terrific last night."

"What about the party?"

"It's okay, I guess, only no drinking. And no bothering the pigeons. People have to park somewhere else. I'm not telling Hattie." Instead, she'd say she was going to a party at Lana's.

"How nice you're going to a party," Hattie said, predictably, and baked two dozen chocolate cupcakes for her to take, each one with a letter dripped on the white icing in chocolate, the whole of it spelling "Happy Graduation Class of '99." Hattie's concept of a party hadn't changed since the birthday parties Hattie and Mom had given her when she was a kid.

"Thanks, Hattie. They match the Ice Cream Sundae wall."

Oops, that was almost a slip.

Lana, Jim, and Trent got there early, carrying a sound system, CDs, coolers, and card tables even before Robin closed the shell shop to the public. She was still in her jeans and T-shirt from working all day. She emptied the cash drawer and left Lana in charge to go home to change.

"Remember, Lana, no one gets in with alcohol."

When Robin came back, locked the door, and went down, at each turn in the stairway the rock music blared louder, as though she was stepping into an echo chamber. She carried the cupcakes into the party, sure that no one would notice. No one did. She laid them out on a card table in a semicircle around a Coleman lantern. The platform was filled with people dancing. Others were lounging on inflated mattresses in an unlit area.

She watched Lana weaving between groups, never quite still, full of confidence. People laughed at things Lana said that weren't the least bit funny as far as Robin could tell. She tried to enter in and laugh anyway. It sounded forced.

"Ohmygod," Lana shouted. "It'll all be over in twelve days."

No, Robin thought, for Lana it was just beginning.

To avoid looking alone, she slunk off up the stairs as if she remembered something a perfect hostess must do, but a dozen steps up into the passageway, she stopped. She wasn't the hostess. That was as absurd as the cupcakes. She was just the person who opened the cave. She turned and looked down on her cavern filled with foreigners and the smell of marijuana. She expected some beer would get in, but not this much, and not the pot. Maybe someone she didn't know brought it. Maybe many people did. Maybe even Lana.

She saw a guy carving something into the railing and came back down the stairs. "Would you please not do that?"

"Class of '99. We're going to make a mark on the world."

"I said, don't do that."

He went right on, and she felt the first tremor of helplessness. Her hand went out to stop him.

"Hey, man, that's not cool," Trent said from behind her, and the guy stopped.

Trent smiled at her with understanding and she felt a little better. "Don't mind him. He's out of it," Trent said. "Cool place here."

"Usually ten degrees cooler than outside."

"Clever, Miss Weather Lady. I mean I like it in here."

"So do I."

He led her out to dance.

Reggae. She'd never danced to it, but if you felt music, you could dance to anything. Trent was smiling at her. She relaxed and began to enjoy it.

When they stopped, he asked about the cave. She showed him the side cavern, lighting the terraces and stalactites with her father's flashlight. "My dad called it China's Heartland."

"Cool."

Along the back railing in the semidarkness she said, "Look on that rock ledge. What do you see?"

"A bird?"

"Pigeon. She's sitting on her eggs. Keep looking and you'll see more."

"Cool. I wouldn't have noticed."

For an instant she thought of the little boy at the Ice Cream Sundae wall.

Trent pulled her toward him with his arm around her shoulder, then around her waist. She felt lightheaded, like she was swinging up in a Ferris wheel. She was *interesting* to someone! She told him about bootleggers, smugglers, and Chinese aliens in the cave. She was talking fast now. She told him about the cliff divers, the man who lit himself on fire, and it was only words going out of her, like notes without the feel. She thought she could even tell the horse story without getting that sick feeling, that she would finally find words to say how people didn't value things. The horse. Their own lives. She felt he would understand that. She wanted to know if he would. She was about to start, there in the darkness with his arms around her. She opened her mouth, and he was kissing her, his mouth open too—his lips pressing—him holding her—kissing—pushing out of her mind whatever it was she was going to say. His tongue came into her mouth. She pulled back. His grip on the back of her neck tightened and his tongue came in further.

She pushed away from him. "You've ignored me for four years, you know."

"I could say the same about you, my darlink."

She didn't know what his kissing meant. Was it just for fun? Part of his game? A whim of the moment?

"I was telling you a story. Let me finish."

He tried to interrupt her again, his mouth close on her neck, but she dodged him and launched into the story of the horse. She talked fast, urgently, and watched his face. She said the crowd was ripe for excitement, hooting for something wild to crack open the new century. She felt her hand ball up into a fist. "They whipped that horse across his eyes until they ran with blood and he reared and crashed into the corral fence, running in a circle until he found the opening. Out through the alley of blurred, shouting people, the sting of the whip coming again and again." He was listening. The story was working for *her* now. To test the listener. She'd know about him by how he responded. "They whipped his beautiful chestnut side until he ran like the wind, like Pegasus, and flew off the cliff in a big arc, pawing the air, and broke apart on the rocks below."

She was close enough to see the vein in Trent's temple pulse. Yes, yes, he was feeling it.

"Must have been an old nag ready for the glue factory."

That hit her in the chest with a thud, but she went on, to find out, this time feeling the words, not just saying them—the sea turning red around him, his jaw opening, his throat gagging—in the hope that Trent would feel them too. When she got to the bones lodged in the cave and people collecting them, he said, "Cool. Do you have any?"

There. That was the reason she was telling the story. Right there.

"You missed the whole point. Life's so cheap to people, even a horse's life. You mean to say you'd be one of those people yelling from the cliff?"

Suddenly there was a shout and someone sitting on the front railing fell backward onto the rocks. People laughed at his drunken clumsiness until a wave knocked him down. Another wave banged his head against the rocks and sucked him outward. Robin rushed to that railing and shined the light on him. His eyes were open underwater. Spasms of fear shot through her. A person could have his eyes open underwater and not see anything.

People stopped dancing and came to look. Trent and Jim climbed over the railing to help him, but another huge wave knocked them both down and rammed the guy who'd fallen against the pilings. Trent slipped on the algae but finally hauled up the guy dazed and choking, and everyone cheered.

The party went on.

She was shocked. Someone almost drowned and the party kept right on. Everyone dancing again, rolling on air mattresses, laughing, shouting, teasing the guy who had fallen, daring him to sit on the rail again. He climbed up and stood on it, swaying. "Stoned out of his skull," someone shouted, and everyone laughed. Others climbed up too, bouncing to the music. Where was Trent? Dripping and laughing at the drunks. He wasn't going to do a thing. Neither was Jim. Where was Lana? In a panic Robin whirled around to look, and on the far cavern wall, two people were scratching, in large letters right through the sunset smear of red iron oxide, *Class of '99 rules*.

She elbowed her way through the crowd, feeling like the horse—smart lash of the whip that made him run, blindly, between ranks of shouting people—that horrible moment when he felt no solid earth beneath his hooves—the sick, confused recognition that he had made a horrible mistake.

"Stop it!" she shouted. She yanked their arms down. "You're ruining what took ten thousand years to create."

She pushed past them again, back to the CD player and turned it off. In the jarring silence her voice rang out: "Please leave. All of you." An accusatory "you" echoed off the walls.

"Aw, come on," someone shouted.

"What's the big deal?"

"Get *out*! The party's over."

Lana bolted toward her and whispered words Robin couldn't piece together. "Making a mistake...be sorry tomorrow." Robin could only stare at the mutilated wall.

Someone started the music. She turned it off again. "Take everything with you. It's over." People hooted disapproval. "Out!" she screamed, not knowing where the power for such an order came from. No one moved for a long, horrible moment.

Slowly, Lana began to put the CDs back into the box. Grumbling, people climbed down off the railing and picked up their things.

It would separate her from them forever. They started up the long stairs. Lana was going from her—to music and London and the world—and now, since she'd spoiled the party, Lana's party really, she couldn't follow, even in her shadow. Wouldn't follow—even in her imagination. If they were one person, they'd be a great musician—Lana's half had the talent, she had the passion—but as it was, they were both less than great.

Trent carried a cooler up the stairs and stopped to look back at her. A little scowl rumpled his eyebrows. The same little scowl might have been there if he'd been standing at the cliff looking down at the horse.

But that would have been all. She turned away, numb from learning about him.

She fanned her flashlight beam around the platform. Plastic cups of beer, bottles, cans, cigarettes were everywhere. White frosting was smeared over the railings. Three cupcakes had fallen face down where the card table had been.

Still, a little scowl was something. It could have meant he was sorry things went wrong. He could have stayed. She would have liked for him to stay. In that split second when she had the chance, she hadn't said so. He probably wouldn't have. Those were his friends.

She felt small and alone, as if she had come out before she was fully ready into the too-big outer chamber of a huge Nautilus, and the world outside was cold. Right here by the back railing was where he kissed her. It was a kiss full of questions. She was finding the answers just when it all blew apart. She had something now. Something they didn't. Not an accidental talent or a way to make people laugh. It was a way to find out about people. Not exactly a magic wand, but still it was worth *something*.

She hardened herself—telling the story had taught her how—and aimed the light on the ruined wall. It would take most of the next millennium to heal itself. She sat down on the bottom step to watch.

SUSAN VREELAND

THE COLLECTED POEMS OF HAZEL HALL, edited by John Witte. Oregon State University Press, 101 Waldo Hall, Corvallis, OR 97331-6407, 2000, 228 pages, $22 cloth.

Confined to a wheelchair for most of her life, Hazel Hall (1886-1924) spent her days doing needlework, viewing the physical world through a window and a small mirror propped on her windowsill, and writing poetry that transcended her circumstance. Her poetry at its best brings to consciousness the confines of our own petty and self-imposed limitations. Through the frames of her poems we see also the splendor of the human condition, our *all of skies*, our *everything of earth* as she writes in her poem "Frames," which the editor, John Witte, has chosen as the second poem in the volume.

In fact, it is this tension between earth—the physical, and sky—the spiritual and psychological, that gives many of Hall's poems their taut energy. In her poem "Things That Grow," for example, she celebrates things that grow *through the seething soil of garden-beds* and *wander around in the house of their birth*. In it is the joy of earthy exploration and learning *by growing down, / To build with branches in the air*. But the joy is counterbalanced by the poet's final question: *Untaught by earth how could I wake / The shining interest of the sky?* How, indeed. In the eloquence of the question is the answer. What sky would not awaken to that surprising choice of words, *shining interest*? Yet the poignancy of the plea still resonates. Tension is held.

The release often comes in an ecstasy of metaphor. The section of the book entitled "Needlework" contains several illustrations. In these poems the act of creating through embroidery, knitting, crocheting, and sewing informs life, and the needlework pieces themselves become metaphors. However, more significant and more exquisite is Hall's use of the language of her craft to make everything vibrate. The opening lines to "Heavy Threads" are among many examples:

When the dawn unfolds like a bolt of ribbon
Thrown through my window,
I know that hours of light
Are about to thrust themselves into me
Like omnivorous needles into listless cloth,

If your socks are still on, yours are knit tighter than mine.

The editing of this collection is skillfully unobtrusive. Hall's three published books—"Curtains," "Walkers," and "Cry of Time"—are left intact. "Curtains," which I think has the strongest poems, is further divided into three sections. The last, "Spring from a Window," has only four poems, each about April, but the selection and placement of these particular poems show the editor's good hand. Through these four poems, separated from the others as if by a velvet rope, we see Hall's rhythmic response to her life: Joy, Defiance, Joy, Sorrow. It is a rhythm of inhalation and exhalation, of relaxation and tension. It is the needle in and the needle out of her craft.

This same stress/unstress rhythm of the iamb predominates in her poems. So much so that sometimes I would find myself tiring of the neat iambic, lulled by the steady three- and four-stressed lines. I would find myself approaching the poems like a stale lover. Then I'd turn a page and read a poem that would take my breath away, and I'd be, suddenly, in love again.

Alice Ann Eberman

Editors' Note: The Collected Poems of Hazel Hall *published by OSU Press is part of their Northwest Readers Series. Hall's three books, published to critical acclaim in the 1920s but now out of print, are collected together for the first time in this edition. The poems by Hazel Hall on pages 49, 50, and 51 are taken from this book.*

REACH, *Janet E. Aalfs*. Perugia Press, PO Box 108, Shutesbury, MA 01072, 1999, 86 pages, $11.95 paper.

One of the lovely qualities shared by the poems in Janet Aalfs' book, *Reach*, is a kind of light persistence. The opening sequence is a group of poems titled after movements in Liangong, Chinese healing and strengthening exercises. Aalfs is a martial artist as well as a poet, and she touches on moments of revelation and despair with the delicate sureness of someone used to focusing, stretching, and kicking every day. In "Bleeding the Radiators," she writes of a stuck valve:

...I've come to accept
the work of one who must
time after time return

to the jammed bolt
without a clue. And to the savor
of common grit. And to aspirations

of belief in a hidden
current, joint I'll unlock someday
into the next blazing form.

Aalfs is working with the repetitive motions of body, memory, family, and love. Revealed amidst quotidian details of tomato slices, wind, and combed hair is a girl afraid in her family, who *opens her mouth full / of punishment / soap slathered on her / tongue.* There is a brother who, watching Lassie, *kissed the screen / dog's face and left / a splotch on the glass*; and a mother who sucked secret powers from boiled turkey necks. "The Girl Who Fear Does Not Break" is a strong presence, even when a poem ends with her *mind crouched frozen inside / our father's heavy steps.* In school when she fishes with magnets for paper-clipped words, it is through force of will she catches *sun.*

The adult poet is a strong presence as well. Her poems are full of grasses, waters, and leaves, combined with a mind inclined toward wonder. At dusk, holding her hands in the air, she sees the color blue rising from her skin like satin gloves. Aalfs lets a reader feel *waves / of breath washing over / these bones.*

This is an accomplished, mature writer who makes poem after poem into vessels for intricate sensations that seem simple, profound, and inevitable. In "Silver River," one of the strongest poems in the book, the poet effortlessly follows thought's path from the glimpse of a tail glittering *silver as a skewer* as a possum flees under a fence to childhood memory of playing possum, being urged to get out of the back of a car. The poem ends:

C'mon, hurry up, get out. *But I didn't*
budge, though my heart beat hard, watery
dark
from the silver river washing through me.

The poems become lessons about what washes through a heart, how *memory / pours like apples from a basket*, about how discipline becomes a habit like breath. They hold much pain and human error, but they also arch with spirit, with a child's heart beating rivers, with a woman pushing her palms in four directions.

The poems are not didactic. Rather, like a child in one of the poems from the Liangong series, they bend *low / like a branch offering peaches.* There is a sense throughout these poems that grace both cannot and must be earned.

Susan Stinson

FEELING AS A FOREIGN LANGUAGE: THE GOOD STRANGENESS OF POETRY, *Alice Fulton*. Graywolf Press, 2402 University Ave., Ste. 203, St. Paul, MN 55114, 1999, 303 pages, $15 paper.

In the Preamble to this collection of essays and critical reviews on poets and poetry, Alice Fulton, author of four books of poetry and Professor of English at the University of

Michigan at Ann Arbor, defines the *good strangeness* of language. She believes that *each poet creates an expatriate space, a slightly skewed domain where things are freshly felt because they are freshly said.* She also makes her case for the *eccentric*, thus establishing her criteria for good poetry, recognized in the *shimmer and presence of the..."uncanny."*

Given Fulton's views on the revelatory powers of fresh language, it is not surprising that she devotes a lengthy essay to the poetry of Emily Dickinson, for whom she coined the phrase *feeling as a foreign language*. Fulton observes that of all poets Dickinson best expresses the inexpressible, *the blanks of sentience: emotions so inconvenient they go unnamed.* The other major critical piece included in this volume is an essay on the seventeenth century English poet Margaret Cavendish, an eccentric much reviled by her contemporaries for her unconventional behavior in society as well as her feminist poems. My favorite among Fulton's welcome excerpts from Cavendish's poems is one on hunting, told from the viewpoint of the prey (a rabbit) and concluding in a scathing dressing-down of the "sport" and its practitioners.

The opening piece in the volume demonstrates that in Fulton's hands prose can be as full of surprises as poetry. Entitled "Screens: An Alchemical Scrapbook," it is written as a series of journal entries that meditate on "screens" of all kinds—including veils, beards, and computer screens—with the idea that all screens are *invested with the power of entry and exclusion:*

> *Men have natural veils, beards, which come from within and are painstakingly removed every day. Female veils are imposed from outside; they are cultural rather than natural: makeup. Women want to appear transparent though they are veiled: makeup tries to be invisible.*

Almost in passing, while relating a tragic family story in "Screens," Fulton exemplifies male authority in this vivid passage:

> *In 1977, I almost passed out while trying to make a case for my aunt with her psychiatrist over the phone. "But my dear little girl..." he said, and the patriarchal maw of medical authority seemed to devour all the oxygen in the room.*

Throughout the book Fulton takes every opportunity to comment on the condition of women. In addition to the essays on Dickinson and Cavendish, she features the work of several women poets in the sixty-page section devoted to reviews of books of poetry, some by today's best-known poets and some by poets less well known.

Every age deserves its own poetics. Fulton, in the section "Poetics," proposes some ways of looking at contemporary poetry based on ideas from mathematics and science. From chaos theory the term *fractals* is borrowed to replace the old and inadequate "free verse," and some propositions for new ways of analyzing poetry based on its internal structures. Ideas about the instability of the universe and their connections to the structures and content of poetry have their source in quantum physics.

In the essay "To Organize a Waterfall" Fulton discusses her poem "Cascade Experiment," likening its cause-and-effect logical structure to a scientific experiment by the same name. This is an interesting exercise in fresh vision; however, I don't find a significant difference between the structure of this poem and the periodic structures of Milton's poetry, or Shakespeare's, not to mention countless poems by lesser-known poets of the sixteenth and seventeenth centuries who were trained in classical rhetoric. Nor do I see how the poem differs from the self-qualifying poems of Wallace Stevens, a poet also interested in turning over in language multiple variations on an idea. But these are minor cavils.

In the volume's final essay Fulton explains what is wrong with the poetry of the *dominant culture* today and what she wants from the poems of the future. Framing the ethical role of poetry in terms of our cultural obsession with political correctness, which we carry to absurd lengths in the letter and still fail to practice in the spirit, she calls for a *true* p.c., which she defines as the practice of radical humanism. For poets this would amount to a kind of fearless *mindfulness*. It would require courage to go against the tide of the purely personal in the content of one's poem, which Fulton thinks has become narcissism, seeking instead a poetry of commitment to the great issues of our age; to resist the bland, plain language of the poetry academy as the only *sincere* style; to look to other disciplines for inspiration; and finally, always to seek in one's poems to *transcend* received ideas and emotions.

Fulton's models for transcendence are Emily Dickinson and John Keats. Dickinson is Fulton's poet who transcends emotion by expressing the moments when language often fails. Keats is singled out among the English Romantics, for whom transcendence was a goal, as the poet of constant revision during the course of a poem. Using Keats' "Ode on a Grecian Urn," she argues convincingly that the poet transcends his own stated aesthetic ("Cold Pastoral!") by his insistent questioning of it throughout the poem.

All in all, this collection offers a provocative and wide-ranging selection by a writer whose fresh and eccentric prose is the true *praxis* of her ideas about language. Graywolf Press must also be commended for producing a handsome and readable book. For twenty-five years Graywolf, an independent and, let us hope, not endangered species, has published distinctive volumes of poetry, fiction, and essays in editions that are as satisfying to hold in the hands as they are to read. *Feeling as a Foreign Language* continues in that noble tradition.

Sandra Cookson

I COULD TELL YOU STORIES: SOJOURNS IN THE LAND OF MEMORY, Patricia Hampl. W.W. Norton & Company, 500 Fifth Ave., New York, NY 10110-0017, 1999, 239 pages, $23 cloth, $12.95 paper.

Patricia Hampl has written two previous memoirs that give glimpses of her life and thoughts—*A Romantic Education* and *Virgin Time*. In her most recent book, *I Could Tell You Stories*, she explores memory and imagination as they relate to writing memoirs. In the prologue to *I Could Tell You Stories*, she explains that the book moves between memoirs with stories that tell about the writing of a life and her experience as a reader *trying to tease out from the works of others the habits of memory as it flares into the imagination*.

She explains that inventing details, keeping secrets, and placing oneself within an historical context are essential tools of the memoir genre. Invention occurs because the writer's point of view is subjective, and in trying to recall specific details of an incident or a conversation, the words, shapes, and colors that set the scene and form the atmosphere often are filtered through the writer's own experiences and beliefs.

After recreating the scene of her first piano lesson with Sister Olive Marie, Hampl confesses that she isn't certain that the nun's name was Olive. However, she is sure that her complexion was *olivelike*. She remembers the nun's face gleaming *as if it had just been rolled out of a can and laid on the white plate of her broad, spotless wimple.* She considers the piano lesson incident to be a mystery waiting to be solved. My *narrative self (the culprit who invented) wishes to be discovered by my reflective self, the self who wants to understand and make sense of a half-remembered moment....*

In Hampl's chapter about Walt Whitman's work, she writes of her disillusionment with the government during the Vietnam War years. Reading Whitman's accounts of his Civil War experiences and of his faith in the idea that *alienation under the mantle of individualism* can be *transfigured into a rich and radiant ideal of nationhood* causes her to believe that the nation will be whole again after the war is over.

Ironically, the war ends without victory, and the country remains unsettled over military and social issues. Hampl's idealism drops away. By 1973, she isn't reading Whitman anymore. Instead, she has accepted his invitation to examine her own self and write her own book.

What Hampl gleans from Czeslaw Milosz's writing contrasts with Whitman's admonition to examine oneself. A Polish poet who won a Nobel Prize in 1980, Milosz considers himself to be an instrument for revealing historical events and places his nation's story in the foreground as he narrates incidents from his life.

Coming from Eastern Europe where whole villages have been massacred and national boundaries have been redrawn within a generation, Milosz's fate has been influenced by political events. As he recalls his progress from Poland to California, he uses the tools of his poetic craft: *to see and describe*. Hampl admires his method. She states: *In both lyric poetry and the memoir the real subject is consciousness in the light of history.*

Milosz states that it is not necessary to tell all the particulars of one's fate. Secrets can stay hidden. Hampl quotes Milosz:

The passing over of certain periods important for oneself, but requiring too personal an explanation, will be a token of respect for those undergrounds that exist in all of us and that are better left in peace....

Edith Stein, author of *Life in a Jewish Family*, demonstrates the keeping of a secret that is an integral part of one's self. Although she felt it necessary by 1933 to leave a record of growing up in Judaism that exposed the false picture of Jewish life put forward by the Nazis, she never gave the reason for her conversion to Catholicism in 1922. In 1933 Stein became a Carmelite postulant and in 1942 she died in Auschwitz. (She was canonized in 1998.) Stein's inner enlightenment remains a secret that time has swallowed—*gone now with her into the gray mid-century smoke she became*, Hampl states.

While preparing a review of the *"Definitive Edition" of Anne Frank's Diary* in 1995, Hampl researched a reference to a radio broadcast that Gerrit Bolkestein, Education Minister of the Dutch Government in exile, delivered from London. He urged the Dutch population to collect ordinary documents such as letters and diaries that would leave a history of the Nazi occupation for future generations.

From her family's hiding place in Amsterdam, Anne Frank listened to the broadcast and wrote in her diary the next day that *ten years after the war people would find it very amusing to read how we lived, what we ate, and what we talked about as Jews in hiding.* In her review, Hampl had aimed to place the book in public history and to confirm that Anne Frank had accomplished her mission of showing future readers how she and her family lived during Nazi occupation. She relates a story about a piece of hate mail she received after its publication.

Hampl also explores memory and imagination in the work of Sylvia Plath and in

Augustine's *Confessions*, as well as in many personal stories. Reading Hampl's work inspires a thoughtful state of mind. Following her twists and turns of explanation is like ambling through a maze. But it is a worthwhile journey for those who write memoirs. Hampl defends the genre and gives relevant examples by weaving scenes of her own life into the text. Using her imagination, she sorts through threads of memory, enhancing chosen details and withholding others, but always placing events within a context of history.

Marie Krohn

GIRL IN HYACINTH BLUE, Susan Vreeland. MacMurray & Beck, Alta Court, 1490 Lafayette St., Ste. 108, Denver, CO 80218, 1999, 242 pages, $17.50 cloth.

Susan Vreeland's second novel, *Girl in Hyacinth Blue*, consists of eight tightly connected stories tracing the journey back through the centuries of an imaginary Jan Vermeer portrait: a young woman in a blue smock, sitting in profile in front of a window. The first six stories, more or less portraits of the painting's many owners, are richly drawn, widely varying and very satisfying, but it is the last two stories that take *Girl in Hyacinth Blue* into the realm of extraordinary achievement. Vreeland rejects the myth of the isolated, independent male artist, who manages to create great art in spite of the daily domestic demands of wife, children, and household. Vreeland refuses to minimize the struggles of Vermeer's wife and children; instead, she shows us a man recognizing his debt to those who are most important to his art.

> *In a sudden movement his wife rushed over to take away Geertruida's glass of milk. "No, leave it, Catharina. Right there in the light. It makes the whole corner sacred with the tenderness of just living." In the arranging of these things he felt a pleasure his selfishness surely didn't deserve. He stepped back and breathed more slowly, and what he saw, lit by warming washes of honey and gold, was a respite in stillness from the unacknowledged acts of women to hallow home. That stillness today, he thought, might be all he would ever know of the Kingdom of Heaven.*

Though it uses male protagonists in about half of the stories, the novel never loses sight of the centrality of female experience and the primacy of daily life. *Girl in Hyacinth Blue* necessarily questions the male gaze, but it's more concerned with female choice and action and with the possibility that that gaze can be transformed into something worthy and unthreatening. It's a somewhat weighty message, but *Girl in Hyacinth Blue* carries its serious insights with grace, in a lyrical prose style. Like a Vermeer portrait, where life is suspended in still life, it's the small, reflective moments that are important, as in "Adagia," when a father makes the difficult decision to give the portrait to his newly engaged daughter: *Studying the beauty of her cheek so that he would remember it in twenty years, he motioned her toward him.*

The powerful presence of the "Girl in Hyacinth Blue," as mercurial as she is steady, becomes a catalyst for the action in each story. The mystery of the young woman's identity and state of mind and her spiritual beauty that transcends the merely visual invest the portrait with the power to give hope. Everyone who possesses the painting sees in her the possibilities and questions posed by their own lives, as when a young Jewish girl, more aware than the adults around her of what is about to be swept away by the occupying Nazi army, reflects:

> *Now it became clear to [Hannah] what made her love the girl in the painting. It was*

> *her quietness. A painting, after all, can't speak. Yet she felt this girl, sitting inside a room but looking out, was probably quiet by nature, like she was. But that didn't mean that the girl didn't want anything, like Mother said about her. Her face told her she probably wanted something so deep or so remote that she never dared breathe it but was thinking about it there by the window. And not only wanted. She was capable of doing some great wild loving thing. Yes, oh yes.*

The portrait changes the lives of its owners, and the intent and richness of the novel lie in how each successive story reveals a little more about the one that preceded it. The result is a diverse history of Dutch life from the present time back to the seventeenth century. When the *crazy witch girl* of "From the Personal Papers of Adrian Kuypers" scoffs at her lover, a rationalist windmill engineer, saying, *It doesn't matter how [dikes] work. When the waterwolf wants to come up over those dikes, he's going to, and no pile of mud and seaweed is going to stop him*, we know how true that is, having just read of a great and terrible flood in "Morningshine." One of the most realized and insightful of the novel and my personal favorite, "Morningshine" speaks strongly of and for women's presence and desires. A young farm wife, hungry for beauty in her stark life of work and worry, hopes desperately to keep the painting for her own sake, even as she believes it to be a portrait of the mother of the foundling who came wrapped with it in a shawl, and in the face of her (equally desperate) husband's insistence that they sell it for seed money and food for their own two children:

> *She held Jantje up to the painting. "See, Jantje, how beautiful she is. Maybe this is your mother. See how young she looks? A fine lady in a fine home." If that was so, Jantje had to know that his mother wore blue. The shawl was not blue enough. Besides, it was old and torn. He needed the painting. It wasn't only Jantje who needed the painting. The Oriental tapestry on the table, the map on the wall, the engraved brass latch on the window—since Saskia couldn't have these things in reality, then she wanted them all the more in the painting.*

Vreeland's strength as a writer lies not only in technical skill but in emotion and immediacy, evoked anew in each story, as the boundaries between the painting and life blur and dissolve. It's odd, perhaps, that a painting of an interior, a room, should so often be used to evoke the beauty of nature and the Dutch countryside, but it works. The predominant blue of the painting, Vreeland suggests, is *the blue of hyacinths and Delftware and all fine things*, the blue of Holland and of Dutch life itself. Vreeland uses her characters' varying levels of privilege to show Holland in all its aspects.

Balanced with these glimpses into the complicated joy and pain of ordinary lives, the question of the girl in hyacinth blue's true identity lingers throughout, and the final story, "Magdalena Looking," offers a more than satisfying answer. The painting's subject at last gets her turn to speak, to show that she has her own difficult desires and choices to make. In some ways, the *Girl in Hyacinth Blue* turns out to be what some think her to be. Most significantly though, she, like the novel, embodies an undeniable and arresting spirituality.

Marianna Wright

CONTRIBUTORS' NOTES

KATHERINE ACE lives in Portland (OR). Her artwork is on the covers of magazines, books, and journals nationally and internationally, and her work is included in numerous private, corporate, and public collections.

FRANCES PAYNE ADLER is the Director of the Creative Writing and Social Action Program at California State University (Monterey Bay). The author of several books, including *Raising the Tents* (CALYX Books), she is published widely, including in the *Women's Review of Books*, *Ms. Magazine*, and the *Progressive*.

KATHLEEN ALCALÁ has published four books—*Mrs. Vargas and the Dead Naturalist* (CALYX Books), a collection of short stories, and three novels: *Spirits of the Ordinary*, *The Flower in the Skull*, a Western States Book Award winner, and *Treasures in Heaven* (all Chronicle and Harvest). She is a co-founder of *Raven Chronicles*.

DIANE LILLIAN AVERILL's first book, *Branches Doubled Over with Fruit* (University of Central Florida Press) and her newest collection, *Beautiful Obstacles* (Blue Light Press), were both finalists for Oregon Book Awards. Her work is widely published.

JANE BAILEY is the recipient of an Oregon Arts Commission fellowship in poetry and the C. Hamilton Bailey fellowship in poetry from Oregon Literary Arts. Her poetry is published in *CALYX Journal*, *Poetry Northwest*, and *SLANT*, among others.

ELLEN BASS received the *Nimrod*/Hardman's Pablo Neruda Prize for Poetry. BOA Editions will publish her newest poetry collection in 2002. She teaches creative writing in Santa Cruz (CA) and is the author of *Courage to Heal*.

DEBORAH BYRNE is an editor and has won awards including a Grolier Poetry Prize, the Edgar Allen Poe Award, and the Michael Gerhardt Award. Her poetry is published in *Paterson Review*, *Cold Drill*, and *Salamander*, among others.

CLAUDIA CAVE's paintings have been exhibited in many solo and group exhibitions in galleries and museums thoughout the U.S. and are included in many private and corporate collections. She earned an MFA from the University of Idaho and lives in Corvallis (OR).

SANDRA COOKSON is a Professor of English at Canisius College (Buffalo, NY). She has published numerous articles and book reviews on women writers. Her poems are published in *Pasager* and *Karamu*, among other publications.

SHELLY CORBETT received her BA in Photography from the University of Washington (Seattle). Her art is published on covers of several books, including two CALYX books. She has solo and group exhibits in Washington, New York, California, and Mexico.

KRISTINA KENNEDY DANIELS earned a BFA degree from Ohio State University. She has been painting and drawing for thirty-five years and lives in Corvallis (OR). Her art is published on covers of several books, including several CALYX books, and she is a CALYX art editor.

CORTNEY DAVIS is the author of a poetry book, *Details of Flesh* (CALYX Books), and a new nonfiction narrative—*I Knew a Woman: The Experience of the Female Body* (Random House). Her poetry is published in *Poetry*, *Ontario Review*, and *Prairie Schooner*.

ALICE DERRY teaches English and German at Peninsula College in Port Angeles (WA) and co-directs the Foothills Writers Series. She is the author of two books of poetry:

Stages of Twilight (Breitenbush Books) and *Clearwater* (Blue Begonia Press). A third, *So, You're German?* is forthcoming from Louisiana State University Press.

Monique De Varennes earned an MA from the Writing Seminars at Johns Hopkins. Her first short story was published in *The Virginia Quarterly Review*. She lives in Los Angeles.

Jasmine Donahaye is a student at the University of California, Berkeley, where she is studying Celtic Studies, with a minor in Creative Writing. She moved to the United States from England ten years ago.

Alice Ann Eberman taught literature and creative writing at Crescent Valley High School (Corvallis, OR) for over twenty years. Her poetry is published in *CALYX Journal*, *Fireweed*, and *From Here We Speak: An Anthology of Oregon Poetry* (OSU Press).

M. Evelina Galang is the author of *Her Wild American Self* (Coffee House Press). The collection's title story has been short listed by Best American Short Stories and received a Pushcart Prize. She is working on a novel, *What is Tribe*, and teaches creative writing at Iowa State University.

Iggi Green's work is widely exhibited in solo and group exhibitions throughout the Northwest. She earned a BA from The Evergreen State College (Olympia, WA).

Annette Gurdjian's work has been shown in solo and group exhibitions throughout the Northwest, Idaho, Massachusetts, North Carolina, Wisconsin, and California. She earned a BFA from the University of Oregon (Eugene) and lives in Eugene.

Hazel Hall (1886-1924) spent most of her life confined to a wheelchair. She was the author of three books of poetry: *Curtains*, *Walkers*, and the posthumous *Cry of Time*. She was born in St. Paul (MN) and died in Portland (OR).

Jennifer Stabler Holland grew up in Palouse County (WA). She earned a degree in Fine Arts from Washington State University (Pullman). Her work is widely exhibited and included in many public collections.

Betsy Johnson-Miller is the mother of two children. She teaches persuasion and public speaking at Eastern Illinois University and has worked an associate pastor.

Belinda Kremer is a native Californian living in Brooklyn, New York. She earned an MFA in poetry at the University of Michigan in Ann Arbor and works as a poet, teacher, and freelance editor.

Marie Krohn lives in Neligh (NE) with her husband, two cats, and two dogs. She's a writer, a pianist, an avid reader, and a gardener. She left a teaching career in 1984 to begin her lifelong dream of writing and is published in several journals and newspapers.

Betty LaDuke is professor of art emeritus at Southern Oregon University (Ashland). She is the author of *Compañeras: Women, Art and Social Change in Latin America* (City Lights, 1986) and *Africa: Women's Art, Women's Lives* (Africa World Press, 1997).

Diana Ma is published in *The Asian Pacific Journal* and *Vox Populi: 1999 Seattle Poetry Festival Anthology*. She earned an MA in creative writing from the University of Illinois, Chicago, and teaches at North Seattle College and Shoreline Community College.

Elizabeth McLagan lives in Portland (OR) and Spokane (WA) and was a founding editor of *CALYX Journal*. She is published in *Willow Springs* and *Barnabe Mountain Review* as well as in the anthologies *Portland Lights* and *Essential Love*.

Chi Meredith is a painter and printmaker who lives in Corvallis (OR). Her work is widely exhibited and is published in *CALYX Journal*, *Science and Other Way of Knowing*, *Southwest Art Magazine*, and *Women of Power*.

Ilze Klavina Mueller is a native of Latvia. She is a poet, translator, interpreter, and language teacher who has made her home in Minnesota for the past twenty-six years. Her work and translations are widely published.

Tamara Musafia works at Oregon State University (Corvallis) as a research assistant. She is the mother of two children. Born in Sarajevo, the war in Yugoslavia is her own personal tragedy.

Jane Orleman is published in numerous journals and magazines including *Woman's Journal*, *The Northwest Review*, and *CALYX Journal*. Her work is widely exhibited in the Northwest and across the country.

Janine H. Oshiro is a Hawaii-born writer, barista, and karaoke junkie currently living in Portland (OR). She is a self-described dropout of *The Artist's Way* and is an interminable creator of poems, stories, comics, dolls, and smiles.

Monique Passicot was born in Buenos Aires, Argentina. She has a long list of exhibitions, is an illustrator of children's books, and has had work featured in several art journals and catalogs.

Sheri Rice studied at the San Francisco Center for the Book and teaches art to youth. Her work is widely exhibited and is published in *CALYX Journal*, *Pasadena Star News*, the *Marin County Independent Journal*, and the *San Francisco Examiner*.

Lois Rosen teaches English as a second language at Chemeketa Community College (Salem, OR). Her work is published in *Writer's Forum*, *Hubbub*, *Fireweed*, and *Northwest Review*.

Manya Shapiro's work is exhibited throughout the country and is included in public collections in Oregon and Washington. She has worked on set designs for Portland State University, The Elizabeth Leach Gallery, and The Portland Art Museum.

Susan Stinson is the author of two novels, *Martha Moody* and *Fat Girl Dances with Rocks*. She has recently completed a new manuscript, *Venus of Chalk*. Her work is published in *Kenyon Review*, *Seneca Review*, *Yellow Silk*, and *Curve*, among others.

Anita Sullivan tunes pianos in Corvallis (OR) and has published two essay collections on her craft. She is the author of a chapbook of poems, *I Hear the Crickets Laughing* (Howlet Press), and is working on too many writing projects at once.

Angelita Surmon was born in Lebanon (OR) and received her BS and BFA degrees from Oregon State University. She lives in southeast Portland with her husband Marc, their eight-year-old daughter, Elena, and yellow lab, Emma.

Joanna Thomas is a multi-media artist working in a variety of techniques. Her work is exhibited in Florida and is represented by the Amby Edinger Gallery in Ellensburg (WA) and the Simon Edwards Gallery in Yakima (WA).

Gail Tremblay, of Onondaga/Micmac and French Canadian ancestry, has published three poetry books, including *Indian Singing* (CALYX Books). Her writing is widely published and translated and her visual art is widely exhibited. She teaches at The Evergreen State College (Olympia, WA), where she grows a wonderful garden.

MARINA TSVETAEVA (1892-1941) was born in Moscow, where her first collection of poetry was published in 1910. She lost her daughter and husband to Stalin's Soviet prison system. For many years her work appeared only in foreign and underground publications. This is the first publication in English of the complete "Insomnia." **KRISTIN BECKER (TRANSLATOR)** has taught English and writing. She received her MFA from Syracuse University where she won the Harriet Wilson Jaycox/Rubaiyat Poetry Group Prize. She is published in *CALYX Journal* and *Poetry Motel*, among others.

SUSAN VREELAND's novel-in-stories, *Girl in Hyacinth Blue* (MacMurray & Beck), received starred reviews from *Publishers Weekly*, *Kirkus*, and *Booklist* and was a BookSense '76 selection. Her short fiction is widely published.

JUDITH WERNER lives in New York City. She is published in several anthologies and magazines, including *The South Dakota Review*, *ELF*, *Slant*, *Riverrun*, *Bridges*, *Yankee*, *The Lyric*, *Lullwater Review*, and *Rattapallax*, where she is Senior Editor.

ELAINE WINER is the recipient of numerous literary awards and is published in *Tropic*, *Sunshine*, and *Etcetera*. She divides her time between Miami Beach, Nantucket, and Morristown.

MARIANNA WRIGHT received her MA in English from the University of Washington (Seattle), and now lives in Wisconsin, where she volunteers at a rape crisis center and works for the state.

EDITORS' NOTES

LOIS CRANSTON was a CALYX editor for ten years. Born in 1923 on her parents' farm in Kettle Falls, WA, she was taught to love both literature and the natural world. She repaired aircraft instruments and was a welder during WWII in Oregon and worked in the health and social services fields in California until she retired in 1985 and moved to Corvallis where two of her six children live.

KRISTINA KENNEDY DANIELS received a Bachelor of Fine Arts degree from The Ohio State University. She has been painting and drawing for thirty-five years, and she has been an art editor for CALYX for over twenty years.

MARGARITA DONNELLY, a founding editor of CALYX, is the Director. She co-edited *The Forbidden Stitch: An Asian American Women's Anthology* (American Book Award winner) and other CALYX anthologies. She is the recipient of a Fishtrap Writing Fellowship and the inaugural Distinguished Achievement Award from the OSU Friends of the Library. She was born and raised in Venezuela.

LOUISE LAFOND was born and raised in central Minnesota. She earned a BA in art at the College of St. Benedict (St. Joseph, MN) and an MFA at the University of Wisconsin, Madison. LaFond taught drawing, design, and printmaking at Colorado College in Colorado Springs. Her work is exhibited widely and included in many public and private collections. LaFond has been a CALYX art editor since 1992.

BEVERLY MCFARLAND became a CALYX editor in 1989 and is the Senior Editor. She earned a Bachelors of Journalism and a BA in English from the University of Texas, Austin, and an MAIS in English, Journalism, and Education from Oregon State University (Corvallis). She co-edited *A Line of Cutting Women*. She is married to a fellow ex-Texan, and they have three grown children.

MICKI REAMAN moved to Corvallis for a CALYX internship in 1992 and became a CALYX editor and a staff member soon after. She is the Managing Editor. She co-edited *Present Tense: Writing and Art by Young Women* and *A Line of Cutting Women*. She earned a BA in contemporary literature and feminist theory from The Evergreen State College (Olympia, WA).

CHRISTINE RHEA has been a CALYX editor since 1995. She coordinates the advocacy program in a victim assessment center for children. Volunteer activities include editing a community newsletter and developing a variety of outreach web pages for local nonprofit groups. She has a BA from Radford University (VA) and is a veteran of the U.S. Army.

CAROLYN SAWTELLE has been in the graphics/printing field for over twenty years, working as a designer, production artist, and supervising the graphics department of a printing company. She has volunteered at CALYX since 1987 in various capacities, currently as a Journal art editor. Her spare time is spent quilting and developing an interest in woodworking.

Linda Varsell Smith teaches creative writing at Linn-Benton Community College. She was on the boards of the Oregon State Poetry Association and Willamette Literary Guild. A CALYX editor since 1982, she oversees poetry contests at the Benton County Fair, produced the *Eloquent Umbrella* (LBCC's creative arts journal), published poetry, and is working on ten fantasy novels. She is a doting grandmother.

Sharilyn Smith lives in Corvallis, on the edge of the Cascadia bioregion's Range of Rain, where she creates traditional functional pottery, writes poetry, and teaches elementary level ESL. Her poems are published in *CALYX Journal* and *Fireweed: Poetry of Western Oregon*. She was an intern at CALYX and has been an editor since 1999.

SELECTED TITLES FROM AWARD-WINNING CALYX BOOKS

NONFICTION

Natalie on the Street by Ann Nietzke. A day-by-day account of the author's relationship with an elderly homeless woman who lived on the streets of Nietzke's central Los Angeles neighborhood. *PEN West Finalist.*
ISBN 0-934971-41-2, $14.95, paper; ISBN 0-934971-42-0, $24.95, cloth.

The Violet Shyness of Their Eyes: Notes from Nepal by Barbara J. Scot. A moving account of a western woman's transformative sojourn in Nepal as she reaches mid-life. *PNBA Book Award.*
ISBN 0-934971-35-8, $15.95, paper; ISBN 0-934971-36-6, $24.95, cloth.

In China with Harpo and Karl by Sibyl James. Essays revealing a feminist poet's experiences while teaching in Shanghai, China.
ISBN 0-934971-15-3, $9.95, paper; ISBN 0-934971-16-1, $17.95, cloth.

FICTION

Undertow by Amy Schutzer. A vivid and moving exploration of how the body and mind adjust to the powerful currents of lies and love. Finalist, Lambda Book Award.
ISBN 0-934971-76-5, $14.95, paper; ISBN 0-934971-77-3, $29.95, cloth.

The Inner Life of Objects by Maxine Combs. This quirky novel is a romp through the lives of five characters involved in exploration of the paranormal. Together they bring light to the details and beliefs that connect and compel their lives.
ISBN 0-934971-72-2, $14.95, paper; ISBN 0-934971-73-0, $29.95, cloth.

The End of the Class War by Catherine Brady. Eloquent stories explore the lives of working-class Irish American women contending with the holy trinity of the Irish: melancholy, melodrama, and morbid guilt.
ISBN 0-934971-66-8, $13.95, paper; ISBN 0-934971-67-6, $27.95, cloth.

Switch by Carol Guess. Quirky and charming as *Fried Green Tomatoes*. Cartwheel, Indiana, seems normal enough. But through Guess' seemless narrative, a mystical town full of unexpected secrets is exposed.

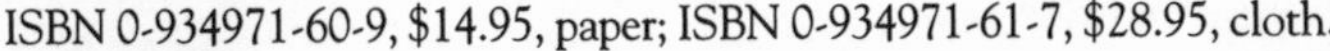
ISBN 0-934971-60-9, $14.95, paper; ISBN 0-934971-61-7, $28.95, cloth.

Four Figures in Time by Patricia Grossman. This novel tracks the lives of four characters in a New York City art school. Grossman reveals the struggles of these very different individuals whose lives coincidentally and irretrievably intersect.
ISBN 0-934971-47-1, $13.95, paper; ISBN 0-934971-48-X, $25.95, cloth.

The Adventures of Mona Pinsky by Harriet Ziskin. In this fantastical novel, a 65-year-old Jewish woman, facing alienation and ridicule, comes of age and is reborn on a heroine's journey.
ISBN 0-934971-43-9, $12.95, paper; ISBN 0-934971-44-7, $24.95, cloth.

Killing Color by Charlotte Watson Sherman. These mythical short stories by a gifted storyteller explore the African-American experience. *Washington Governor's Writers Award*.
ISBN 0-934971-17-X, $9.95, paper; ISBN 0-934971-18-8, $19.95, cloth.

Mrs. *Vargas and the Dead Naturalist* by Kathleen Alcalá. Fourteen stories set in Mexico and the Southwestern U.S., written in the tradition of magical realism.
ISBN 0-934971-25-0, $9.95, paper; ISBN 0-934971-26-9, $19.95, cloth.

Ginseng and Other Tales from Manila by Marianne Villanueva. Poignant short stories set in the Philippines. *Manila Critic's Circle National Literary Award Nominee*.
ISBN 0-934971-19-6, $9.95, paper; ISBN 0-934971-20-X, $19.95, cloth.

POETRY

The Woman of Too Many Days by Mary I. Cuffe. *The Woman of Too Many Days* is a bad accident of a woman who enters your life with a great sideways thrust of her hips and settles into her own rhythm.
ISBN 0-934971-68-4, $12.95, paper; ISBN 0-934971-69-2, $26.95, cloth.

Black Candle: Poems about Women from India, Pakistan, and Bangladesh by Chitra Divakaruni. The author of *Sister of My Heart* reveals, in sumptuous and jeweled language, often forgotten women who quietly bear the burden of generations of pain. *Gerbode Award.* Revised edition.
ISBN 0-934971-74-9, $12.95, paper; ISBN 0-934971-75-7, $26.95 cloth.

Light in the Crevice Never Seen by Haunani-Kay Trask. A revised edition of the first collection of poetry by an indigenous Hawaiian to be published on the mainland, this book is a Native woman's impassioned, lyrical account of her land and people.
ISBN 0-934971-70-6, $12.95, paper; ISBN 0-934971-71-4, $26.95, cloth.

Indian Singing by Gail Tremblay. A brilliant work of hope by a Native American poet. Revised edition, expanded; introduction by Joy Harjo. *Indian Singing* is a visionary quest that presents enduring lessons to accommodate change in troubled times.
ISBN 0-934971-64-1, $11.95 paper; ISBN 0-934971-65-x, $23.95 cloth.

Details of Flesh by Cortney Davis. Nurse-practitioner Davis conducts a frank exploration of caregiving in its many guises: a nurse tending to patients, a woman tending to parents, children, lovers.
ISBN 0-934971-57-9, $11.95 paper; ISBN 0-934971-58-7, $23.95, cloth.

Another Spring, Darkness: Selected Poems of Anuradha Mahapatra translated by Carolyne Wright et al. The first English translation of poetry by this working-class woman from West Bengal.
ISBN 0-934971-51-X, $12.95 paper; ISBN 0-934971-52-8, $23.95, cloth.

The Country of Women by Sandra Kohler. A collection of poetry that explores woman's experience as sexual being, as mother, as artist. Kohler finds art in the mundane, the sacred, and the profane.
ISBN 0-934971-45-5, $11.95, paper; ISBN 0-934971-46-3, $21.95, cloth.

Open Heart by Judith Mickel Sornberger. An elegant collection rooted in a woman's relationships with family, ancestors, and the world.
ISBN 0-934971-31-5, $9.95, paper; ISBN 0-934971-32-3, $19.95, cloth.

Raising the Tents by Frances Payne Adler. A personal and political volume documenting a Jewish woman's discovery of her voice.
ISBN 0-934971-33-1, $9.95, paper; ISBN 0-934971-34-X, $19.95, cloth.

Color Documentary by LuAnn Keener. Here the personal and the political meet with fine, lyric intensity.
ISBN 0-934971-39-0, $11.95, paper; ISBN 0-934971-40-4, $21.95, cloth.

Idleness Is the Root of All Love by Christa Reinig, translated by Ilze Mueller. Poems by the prize-winning German writer accompany two older lesbians through a year together in love and struggle.
ISBN 0-934971-21-8, $10, paper; ISBN 0-934971-22-6, $18.95, cloth.

ANTHOLOGIES

A Line of Cutting Women edited by Beverly McFarland, et al. Spanning community, time, and place, this anthology showcases 37 discoveries from the first 22 years of *CALYX Journal.*
ISBN 0-934971-62-5, $16.95, paper; ISBN 0-934971-63-3, $32, cloth.

Present Tense: Writing and Art by Young Women edited by Micki Reaman, et al. Showcases original work from women linked by their youth but from different sexual orientations, ethnicities, socio-eonomic backgrounds. Contributor Kristin King's story, "The Wings," received a Pushcart Prize.
ISBN 0-934971-53-6, $14.95, paper; ISBN 0-934971-54-4, $26.95, cloth.

The Forbidden Stitch: An Asian American Women's Anthology edited by Shirley Geok-lin Lim, et al. The first Asian American women's anthology. *American Book Award*.
ISBN 0-934971-04-8, $16.95, paper; ISBN 0-934971-10-2, $32, cloth.

Women and Aging, An Anthology by Women edited by Jo Alexander, et al. The only anthology that addresses ageism from a feminist perspective. A rich collection of older women's voices.
ISBN 0-934971-00-5, $15.95, paper; ISBN 0-934971-07-2, $28.95, cloth.

CALYX Books are available to the trade from Consortium and other major distributors and jobbers. CALYX Journal *is available to the trade from Ingram Periodicals and other major distributors.*

CALYX, A JOURNAL OF ART AND LITERATURE BY WOMEN

CALYX Journal,
Volume 18, No. 3

A forum for women's creative work—including work by women of color, lesbian and bisexual women, young women, old women—*CALYX Journal* breaks new ground. Each issue is packed with new poetry, short stories, artwork, photography, and book reviews.

CALYX Journal is recognized for discovering important writers. Writers such as Julia Alvarez, Paula Gunn Allen, Olga Broumas, Natalie Goldberg, Barbara Kingsolver, and Sharon Olds were all published early in their careers in *CALYX Journal*. Recent issues include work from award-winning writers like Rita Marie Nibasa, Juliette Torrez, Kristin King, and Nomy Lamm, a *Ms. Magazine* woman of the year.

CALYX brings the voices and images of over forty women into print with each biannual issue. A three-volume subscription saves over 33 percent off the newsstand price—you'll find the literature of these women is priceless.

As a small non-profit organization, CALYX would be lost without the generous support of volunteers and interns. We always ask interns to comment about their time at CALYX:

Such beauty and strength that CALYX brings to this crazy, crazy world. It was a great honor for me to watch the process and be a part of it.

—Danielle Devore, Intern

My first day at CALYX left the greatest impression on me. Not really knowing what I was doing, I sorted through the mail. Immediately I became completely absorbed in submission after submission—women from all over the country, from all walks of life submitting their work, their words in hopes of being published. I realized then how unique and important CALYX is for giving women an opportunity to have their voices heard.

—Sarin Sephar, Intern

Excerpt: *Cedars* by Pat Cason (Vol. 18:2)

When the air still held your shape
and the blue cotton dress with butterfly sleeves
still wore your scent, I'd slip into it
like your discarded skin,
to inhabit the shape you once held.
My body still wears your absence, wound
that wouldn't subside, stain
as thick as our mother's tears
when she searched through your dresser
for the underwear to bury you in.

Volume 18, No. 2,
Winter 1998/99

I was very excited to come across CALYX in the bookstore. I love the poetry. I love the fiction. I love the power and urgency and honesty of the voices that covered each and every page of your journal.
—S.B., Brooklyn, NY

Volume 18, No. 1, Summer 1998

CALYX *Journal* is published twice yearly. One volume includes three issues. Subscription rates per volume: $19.50 individual; $25 institutional.

Individuals may order books and journal subscriptions or single issues direct from CALYX Books, P.O. Box B, Corvallis, OR 97339. Send check or money order in U.S. currency; add $3.00 postage for first book, $1.00 each additional book. Credit card orders only: FAX to 541-753-0515 or call toll-free 1-888-FEM BOOK.

Colophon

Titles in this book are set in Optima, with body text in Goudy Old Style. Skia was used on the title page.

Typesetting and page layout provided by ImPrint Services, Corvallis, Oregon.